Selections from the *Gespräche* (1655–56) with Capellen

Recent Researches in Music

A-R Editions publishes seven series of critical editions, spanning the history of Western music, American music, and oral traditions.

Recent Researches in the Music of the Middle Ages and Early Renaissance
   Charles M. Atkinson, general editor

Recent Researches in the Music of the Renaissance
   James Haar, general editor

Recent Researches in the Music of the Baroque Era
   Christoph Wolff, general editor

Recent Researches in the Music of the Classical Era
   Neal Zaslaw, general editor

Recent Researches in the Music of the Nineteenth and Early Twentieth Centuries
   Rufus Hallmark, general editor

Recent Researches in American Music
   John M. Graziano, general editor

Recent Researches in the Oral Traditions of Music
   Philip V. Bohlman, general editor

Each edition in *Recent Researches* is devoted to works by a single composer or to a single genre. The content is chosen for its high quality and historical importance and is edited according to the scholarly standards that govern the making of all reliable editions.

For information on establishing a standing order to any of our series, or for editorial guidelines on submitting proposals, please contact:

A-R Editions, Inc.
Middleton, Wisconsin

800 736-0070 (North American book orders)
608 836-9000 (phone)
608 831-8200 (fax)
http://www.areditions.com

RECENT RESEARCHES IN THE MUSIC OF THE BAROQUE ERA, 166

Andreas Hammerschmidt

Selections from the *Gespräche* (1655–56) with Capellen

Edited by Charlotte A. Leonard

A-R Editions, Inc.
Middleton, Wisconsin

Performance parts are available from the publisher.

A-R Editions, Inc., Middleton, Wisconsin
© 2010 by A-R Editions, Inc.

All rights reserved. No part of this book may be reproduced or transmitted in any form by any electronic or mechanical means (including photocopying, recording, or information storage and retrieval) without permission in writing from the publisher.

The purchase of this edition does not convey the right to perform it in public, nor to make a recording of it for any purpose. Such permission must be obtained in advance from the publisher.

A-R Editions is pleased to support scholars and performers in their use of *Recent Researches* material for study or performance. Subscribers to any of the *Recent Researches* series, as well as patrons of subscribing institutions, are invited to apply for information about our "Copyright Sharing Policy."

Printed in the United States of America

ISBN-13: 978-0-89579-686-8
ISBN-10: 0-89579-686-4
ISSN: 0484-0828

∞ The paper used in this publication meets the minimum requirements of the American National Standard for Information Sciences—Permanence of Paper for Printed Library Materials, ANSI Z39.48-1992.

Contents

Acknowledgments   vi

Introduction   vii

   The Composer   vii
   Liturgical Cycles   vii
   Musical Dialogues   viii
   The *Gespräche* of 1655 and 1656: Content and Musical Style   ix
   The Capella Tradition, Michael Büttner, and the Bohn Collection   x
   The Music of the Edition   xi
   Notes on Performance   xiv
   Appendix   xvi
   Notes   xxii

Texts and Translations   xxviii

Plates   xxxi

Selections from the *Musicalische Gespräche über die Evangelia* (1655)
and *Ander Theil Geistlicher Gespräche über die Evangelia* (1656)

   Freue dich, du Tochter Zion   3
   Mein Sohn, warumb hast du uns das gethan?   17
   Herr, ich bin nicht werth   30
   O Herr hilf, wir verderben!   49
   O Vater, aller Augen warten auff dich   74
   Gott fähret auff mit Jauchtzen!   93
   Vater Abraham   121
   Es wird eine grosse Trübsal seyn   142

Critical Report   161

   Sources   161
   Editorial Methods   163
   Critical Commentary   164

Acknowledgments

I acknowledge and thank the work of Desmond Maley, of the J. N. Desmarais Library at Laurentian University, Sudbury, Canada, who served as editor and proofreader of the introduction, and of Howard Weiner, who corrected and improved my German translations. I would like to thank the two libraries that permitted me to publish these pieces: Sächsische Landesbibliothek – Staats- und Universitätsbibliothek, Dresden; and Staatsbibliothek zu Berlin – Preußischer Kulturbesitz. I would also like to acknowledge the research of Barbara Wiermann, who verified Michael Büttner's contribution to the Bohn Collection manuscripts, and of Janette Tilley, whose dissertation proved invaluable in this project.

Introduction

This volume brings together two related collections of Lutheran music from the mid-seventeenth century. First, it provides a modern edition of eight compositions from two popular publications by Andreas Hammerschmidt: the *Musicalische Gespräche über die Evangelia* (Musical Conversations about the Gospels [Dresden, 1655]) and *Ander Theil Geistlicher Gespräche über die Evangelia* (Second Part of the Sacred Conversations about the Gospels [Dresden, 1656]). Second, it adds to these eight works capella parts created by Hammerschmidt's contemporary Michael Büttner (and his copyists) and thus illuminates the performance tradition of adding extra singers and instrumentalists (capellen) to the tuttis of church compositions—a practice common in seventeenth-century Breslau, Silesia (now Wrocław, Poland). This volume not only offers the first modern edition of the eight works of Hammerschmidt, but also is the first publication to combine Hammerschmidt's music with Büttner's added capellen.

The Composer

Andreas Hammerschmidt (1611/12–75) stood second only to Heinrich Schütz (1585–1672) as the most celebrated German composer of the seventeenth century. The quantity and geographic distribution of his original publications and reprint editions attest to his widespread renown.[1] Dedicatory poems—including one by Schütz—demonstrate the level of esteem with which he was regarded in his own time,[2] and references to him appear in dictionaries, treatises, and other musical writings from the seventeenth through twentieth centuries.[3] The paucity of biographical data on Hammerschmidt stands in contrast to his copious output.[4] His duties as organist at Schloss Weesenstein (1633–34), the church of St. Petri in Freiberg (1634–39), and particularly the church of St. Johannis in Zittau (1639–75) did not appear to hinder his compositional activity. Hammerschmidt produced numerous collections of sacred music for voice (both a cappella and with instruments), secular vocal music, instrumental music, and occasional works. Both Martin Fuhrmann's treatise *Musicalischer-Trichter* (1706)[5] and Johann Walther's *Musicalisches Lexicon* (1732)[6] mention Hammerschmidt, indicating that his music was still part of the German sacred repertoire during the eighteenth century. Representative of the praise that Hammerschmidt received posthumously is the following from Johann Bähr's *Musicalische Discurse* (1719):

> He has done more concerning the glory of God than a thousand artists have done or ever will do. He is also the one (this is largely the reason for his immortal fame) who has maintained the music in nearly all village churches to the present day, which a thousand artists with their leaps and contra-fugues have been unable to do; because they wanted only to be noticed and not heard, their capriciousness could not be understood by the simple country folk as easily as Hammerschmidt's work.[7]

Liturgical Cycles

Hammerschmidt aided his fellow church musicians in selecting appropriate weekly repertoire by providing collections of music in liturgical cycles, which offered pieces for the Sundays and principal feast days of the church year. The concept of composing a complete cycle of music for the liturgical year has precedents in such works as the *Magnus liber organi* and Heinrich Isaac's *Choralis Constantinus*.[8] In the Lutheran tradition, musical cycles typically reflected the weekly gospel readings, or pericopes. Indeed, gospel readings were a common means of organizing a varying array of religious matter, ranging from sermons to emblems, into concise, convenient, and easily accessible cycles.[9] Furthermore, these musical cycles may have had a cyclical model in Martin Luther's *Kirchenpostille*, or short commentaries on passages from the Bible. ("Postil" is an abbreviation for "post illa verba textus," or "after those words of the text."[10]) As Hans J. Hillerbrand has noted, these *Postille* were developed "to provide homiletical material to be used by ministers in the exposition of the Gospel."[11]

Since the sermon was normally based on the gospel pericope, and as music was normally performed after the gospel or the sermon, liturgical cycles facilitated the work of the church musician in providing appropriate music that complemented and reinforced the liturgical subject of the day.[12] Already by the mid-sixteenth century, Georg Rhau (1488–1548), who may have had an association with Luther, published collections of motets of the Gospels by various composers for the major feasts of the church year.[13] Eventually composers such as Andreas Raselius (ca. 1563–1602) wrote sets of motets based on the Gospel (sometimes called *Spruchmotetten*[14]) for the entire liturgical year, as well as for the principal feasts.[15] Beyond these sets of motets, seventeenth-century Lutheran composers such as Christoph Demantius (1567–1643) published collections of sacred music for the church year. Demantius, moreover, was likely acquainted with Hammerschmidt in Freiberg and probably provided a model for Hammerschmidt's own liturgical cycles.[16] Yet while many seventeenth-century Lutheran composers published collections of sacred music for the church year, only three composers produced cycles that consisted solely of dialogues: Hammerschmidt (with works from two of these publications presented here)[17] and his contemporaries Johann Rudolf Ahle (1625–73)[18] and Wolfgang Carl Briegel (1626–1712).[19]

Musical Dialogues

Dialogues as musical forms can be traced back to the Easter dialogue "Quem quaeritis."[20] Seventeenth-century definitions of the term dialogue,[21] or *Gespräch*, commence with Michael Praetorius, who in 1619 wrote that "dialogues are familiar to everyone, as a dialogue is a conversation in which a question is encountered and responded to by alternating choirs; echoes fall into this category as well."[22] By placing the description of dialogues in a chapter on secular vocal forms that also included *canzoni, canzonette,* and aria, Praetorius further implied that dialogues were associated with secular music.

While Praetorius suggested that the terms "dialogue" and "echo" may be used interchangeably, Demantius differentiated between the two in a 1656 treatise:

> *Dialogues* are those songs in which several voices answer questions posed by other [voices].... *Echo* is the same as a dialogue, except that the answering voices have to match the preceding ones harmonically for a considerable number of notes at the end of the preceding question, yet they have to be sung in a subdued manner, *piano*, or softly.[23]

Later writers who defined this term followed Demantius's division between dialogue and echo, though with slight modifications. Johann Rudolf Ahle's 1673 definition of echo explicitly allows the use of fewer voices,[24] and Johann Georg Ahle's 1704 revision of his father's treatise leaves these definitions virtually unchanged.[25] In 1706, Fuhrmann further expanded upon prevailing definitions by commenting on the placement of the echoing choir, noting that "a choir positioned in a hidden place performs [an echo] softly."[26] Daniel Speer introduced instruments into the definition in 1697,[27] while Walther went a step further in 1732 with the inclusion of multiple choirs and organ.[28]

In 1739 Johann Mattheson clarified that dialogues are sacred works and that instruments can partake in musical rhetoric:

> The *Dialogi*, or sung conversations . . . have as many types as subjects. They are merely prose discussions on pitches, which are commonly conducted by scriptural persons and are derived either from the Evangelical or other Biblical stories word by word. Their style is somewhat madrigalistic. Their character is historical and devotional, whereby different persons who are conversing are introduced, most often in a long arioso, sometimes with and sometimes without accompaniment. Here are neither true recitatives nor arias, but an uninterrupted alternation of the conversation, without further change, except that the voices tend to combine at the end in either a chorale or another piece . . .
>
> The fact that organs can also imitate such conversations with different manuals, in certain ways, is a very good observation in Walther's dictionary. Such a presentation gives us a new indication that musical rhetoric is also inherent to instruments, and can be made quite intelligible.[29]

Although these definitions offer more or less the same information, their prevalence confirms that these terms were important and perhaps ambiguous enough to warrant definition in the eighteenth century. Common to all dialogues is the alternation of a conversational text in a question-and-answer style between choirs, soloists, instruments, or a combination thereof. Eventually the dialogue became associated only with sacred texts and tended to conclude with a tutti.

Musical dialogues may also be situated within the larger socio-cultural context of the mid-sixteenth through seventeenth centuries, particularly with respect to pedagogical theories and interest in rhetoric, emblems, and meditation.[30] During this period, conversational constructions were a prominent feature of both sacred and secular pedagogical methods. As John Butt has observed, Luther, in his *Small Catechism* (1529), "employs the question-and-answer style in the doctrinal sections and stresses that the pupil (particularly the young) should initially learn both the sacred texts and their commentaries in a single version and alter not a syllable."[31] John W. Doberstein has further noted that Luther's sermons used "direct address, dialogue, and the dramatic form," either by having the characters speak to each other or by creating a dialogue between the preacher and the congregation or doctrinal opponents.[32] This question-and-answer style also appeared in many musical treatises of the period, such as those by Demantius, Johann Rudolf and Johann Georg Ahle, Speer, and Fuhrmann noted above.[33] Another form of didactic treatise includes characterization of teacher and pupil. For example, in Thoinot Arbeau's *Orchésographie* (1589), the conversation concerning dance instruction is between Arbeau and his student Capriol.[34] The familiarity of congregations, schoolboys, and composers with these sorts of didactic models may help account for the popularity of the musical dialogue in the seventeenth century.[35]

Rhetoric was part of the curriculum in both the Latin school and the university,[36] and the concept of persuasion by arousing emotions, engendered through rhetorical techniques, was gaining acceptance during Hammerschmidt's lifetime.[37] As we have already seen, Mattheson implied that dialogues could serve rhetorical purposes by instilling biblical texts in the minds of the congregation, particularly through the use of instruments. More specifically, what makes dialogues so different from other forms of sacred music is the use of texts with first person speech—that is, characterization or personification[38]—a rhetorical device that would have been familiar to any educated person.[39]

In the eight pieces included in this edition, most contain characters speaking the words of the Bible to each other in conversation. Although Hammerschmidt did not label the vocal parts with specific character names, the identities of the speakers would have been clear to a seventeenth-century congregation. For example, in "Mein Sohn, warumb hast du uns das gethan?" three solo voices sing the roles of Joseph (bassus), Mary (cantus), and Christ (altus) in the story of the young Christ in the temple (Luke 2:48–49). Sometimes a duet or ensemble of solo voices represent a group of people, such as the disciples in "O Herr hilf, wir verderben!" who call upon Christ (bassus) to save them from the stormy sea (Matt. 8:25–27).[40] Even in works lacking characterization, concluding tuttis could help draw in the congregation as participants either in the praise of God or in supplication, such as with the final chorale sung in "Es wird eine grosse Trübsal seyn."

The emblem was another popular pedagogical and mnemonic device in seventeenth-century Lutheranism, as groups of emblems organized around the gospels of the day provided a succinct means for pastors and others to study and recall principal elements of the Lutheran faith. Each image (*pictura*) was provided with a title or motto (*inscriptio*) that presented the essence of the subject and a line of poetry or prose (*subscriptio*) that explained the picture.[41] According to Janette Tilley, "the central theme, idea, or saying of the emblem is normally posed as an enigma between the *inscriptio* and the *pictura*," the answer to which is provided by the *subscriptio*.[42] As Tilley suggests, the disposition of the emblem is analogous to that of the musical dialogue, in which a concluding chorus could elucidate the meaning of the earlier parts of the dialogue, offering "a commentary, interpretation, or explanation of the enacted scene" and thereby functioning "as a musical *subscriptio* to the dialogue's *pictura*."[43] In this way, a final tutti also functions much like the final chorus, or *Reyen*, of German baroque drama, which was based on the chorus of Greek tragedy. Indeed, Albrecht Schöne has drawn a similar parallel between emblems and the *Reyen*, observing that "without the chorus the *pictura* of the dialogue remains meaningless, [and] without the dialogue the *subscriptio* of the chorus appears irrelevant. Referring to one another, however, both parts attain their real sense: dialogue and chorus of the tragedy follow the emblematic principle of form."[44]

The choruses of the musical *Gespräche* and dramatic *Reyen* share not only functional similarities, but also formal ones: the chorus is set off from the preceding dialogue through both timbral contrast and metrical change. In the pieces in this edition, Hammerschmidt often changed the meter, usually to $\frac{3}{1}$, for the final tutti; often the text is simply "Alleluia," though in some works a previous text is repeated.

The dialogue is also associated with piety and meditation in seventeenth-century Lutheranism.[45] Literature pertaining to personal, private devotion enjoyed an increase in popularity during the early seventeenth century as theologians sought to improve congregational habits. Many of these publications, such as Johann Gerhard's *Meditationes sacre* (1606), were well received and encouraged meditation.[46] Luther believed that meditation (*meditatio*) was one of three elements necessary to a Christian's life, along with *oratio* (prayer and/or scripture reading) and *tentatio* (the acknowledgement of personal sin and suffering, as well as God's forgiveness through Christ's suffering). Rereading and repeating a text, as well as thinking about it repetitively (*ruminatio*) were essential to meditation.[47] A musical dialogue can incorporate all three of Luther's elements: a scripture reading can be set to a musical phrase that asks for forgiveness and is repeated incessantly.[48] Hammerschmidt's penchant for repetition in works such as "Herr, ich bin nicht werth" may have contributed to some derogatory remarks concerning his musical style,[49] yet it appears that these techniques are supported by rhetorical, pedagogical, and meditative principles.

The *Gespräche* of 1655 and 1656: Content and Musical Style

Together, Hammerschmidt's *Musicalische Gespräche über die Evangelia* and *Ander Theil Geistlicher Gespräche über die Evangelia* (hereafter referred to collectively as the *Gespräche*) provide a complete liturgical cycle. The thirty works from the *Musicalische Gespräche* are listed chronologically in table 1 of the appendix, from the first Sunday of Advent through Pentecost, while the thirty-one works from the *Ander Theil*, shown in table 2 of the appendix, provide music for the remainder of the church calendar, from Trinity Sunday to the twenty-seventh Sunday after. The number of parts and instrumentation in the two publications is similar. The 1655 collection contains works for voices and instruments ranging in size from four to seven parts with continuo, with the majority of pieces more or less equally distributed between five, six, and seven parts. The 1656 collection calls for slightly larger forces, from five to ten parts with continuo, with most compositions in six or seven parts. Between the two collections, six pieces are for voices and continuo only, and just one features a single solo voice. The continuo part in both publications is provided in two figured partbooks, one entitled "Violon *Nach Beliebung*," the other "Continuus"; these two parts are identical, suggesting that Hammerschmidt intended for the bass line to be doubled. In twenty-nine of the sixty-one pieces, the preferred obbligato instruments are two violins, although in five of these, the register calls for violins while the parts indicate cornetins.[50] The majority of the remaining pieces call for many other obbligato instruments, including recorder (*flauto*), cornett (not to be confused with a modern cornet), clarino (or trombetta), trombone, and strings, organized in various combinations. In other words, Hammerschmidt provided the church music director with a variety of works for different combinations of voices and instruments, covering all of the principal Sundays and feast days of the liturgical year.

Of the sixty-one pieces in the two collections, almost all set at least one phrase from the Gospel, usually the gospel of the day. Many of these works combine the Gospel with texts from the Old Testament (usually psalms), another Gospel, another part of the service (such as the doxology), or a chorale verse. Five works in the *Gespräche* that set these other kinds of texts dispense with the Gospel altogether; two of these—"O Vater aller Augen" and "Gott fähret auff mit Jauchtzen!"—are found in this edition with the texts described below.[51] Of the forty-two dialogues identified in the Bible by Michael Märker, twenty-six are represented in part or in full in the *Gespräche*.[52] The majority of Hammerschmidt's dialogues follow the alternating format of a conversational text. Those works using non-dialogic texts often alternate instead between different biblical verses; two of these—"Freue dich, du Tochter Zion" and "Gott fähret auff mit Jauchtzen!"—are included in the present edition.[53]

Hammerschmidt's musical approach to dialogue settings frequently follows the alternating format of a conversational text, but some compositions have lengthy solos for a single voice. The predominance of homophonic textures, conjunct and often reiterative melodies, as well as syllabic, repetitive texts containing few melismas ensure that the words are clearly set, providing for intelligibility in performance. Instruments are used in symphonias, sometimes throughout a work and often in dialogue with the voices. Imitation, while neither strict nor found in every piece, appears between voices, instruments, or voices and instruments. Sectional structures are demarcated by symphonias, refrain-like tuttis, changes in meter, or quasi-polychoral dialogues between one voice and the tutti. Pieces often conclude with a tutti in triple meter and a final cadence in ₵. All of these features are represented throughout the pieces provided in this edition, which are enhanced in a dramatic way when capellen are added.

The Capella Tradition, Michael Büttner, and the Bohn Collection

The tradition of reinforcing vocal and instrumental choirs with additional choirs of voices and instruments, or capellen, has been described elsewhere and thus will be summarized here only briefly.[54] Praetorius stated the following on the subject:

> When à 2.3.4.5.6.7. etc. is found at the head of a vocal concerto . . . it must be understood that the first number means the concertizing voices, the whole foundation of the concerto. The following numbers, however, designate the instrumental or capella voices, which are added only *per accidens, ornatus et plenioris concentus gratiâ* [accidentally, for the sake of a decorated and fuller harmony], as described above, and which can be completely left out if musicians are lacking.[55]

Schütz described two types of choirs—the *Chori Favoriti* and *Capellen*—in the introduction to his *Psalmen Davids* of 1619, explaining that "the former are designated to be 'favored' by the Kapellmeister and used for the finest and most subtle effects, whereas the latter are introduced for strength and magnificence of sound."[56] Later in the baroque period, the meaning of the term had not changed. Johann Andreas Herbst wrote in 1658 that "[a] *capella* is firstly a separate choir, which enters at a certain time in the *clausulis* [cadences, tuttis], like the *ripieno* [voices], to strengthen the music and lend it splendor."[57] Fuhrmann further noted that the capellen "must . . . be placed in a location at a distance from the soloists. In the absence of [sufficient] performers, these capellen can simply be left out, because they [their parts] are in any case also sung by the soloists."[58] Walther defined the capella as "that special or large choir that enters only occasionally for reinforcement and can be called *Chorus ascititius* [supplemental chorus], because it is taken from the other concertizing voices, and extracted."[59] In short, the capella was an additional ensemble that one could add to tutti portions of a work in order to reinforce the solo voices and create a grander, fuller texture.

A paragraph from the foreword to his *Ander Theil* provides a clear link between the capella tradition and Hammerschmidt's *Gespräche*:

> I had in fact intended to extract various *capellen* for most of the pieces of my *Evangelien*; however, since this work has grown appreciably beyond expectation, I have no objection if he whom my work pleases were to extract the same [capellen] where [the music] is full-voiced; and if one has the means, to perform [them] with instruments and doubling voices.[60]

Hammerschmidt also included two identical continuo partbooks for both parts of the *Gespräche*, already suggesting that he wanted to facilitate the addition of capella parts.[61] His call for capellen did not go unheard. A series of capellen created by his contemporary Michael Büttner (1594–1662) and Büttner's copyists supplies extra vocal and instrumental parts to create capellen for the tutti sections of the prints.

Büttner was cantor at St. Maria Magdalena in Breslau from 1634 to 1662. As part of his duties, he gathered the music for the church's library and made arrangements of the music for performance.[62] According to Barbara Wiermann, Büttner modified this music in three ways: (1) composing instrumental sinfonias as preludes and interludes for insertion; (2) creating capellen whereby the extra parts are typically *colla parte* with the original parts; and (3) rewriting a piece to turn it into a polychoral work.[63] The addition of extra sinfonias, instruments, capellen, and choirs, as well as the resulting large ensembles, clarity of formal structure, and strong contrasts, is characteristic of the church music in Breslau at this time.

Büttner's capellen now form part of the Bohn collection, a series of manuscripts that came from the libraries of the three main Protestant churches of seventeenth-century Breslau: St. Elisabeth, St. Maria Magdalena, and St. Bernhardin. According to manuscript analysis done by Wiermann, Büttner was responsible for systematically writing out much of the Bohn collection.[64] Now housed in the Staatsbibliothek zu Berlin – Preußischer Kulturbesitz, the Bohn collection includes music by a number of composers active in Breslau, including Tobias

Zeutschner[65] and Martin Mayer, the latter of whom composed several dialogues.[66] The Bohn collection also contains Büttner's own compositions, including "Der Herr gebe euch vom Thaw deß Himmels," described as a work "auff Dialogen Manier," with twenty-six parts for voices, strings, and brass (including capella), many sinfonias, and time signature changes.[67] Hammerschmidt's music is represented primarily by Ms. mus. 150, which cataloguer Emil Bohn described as a score in organ tablature and single parts.[68] These parts are primarily tutti complements to Hammerschmidt's *Gespräche*, with tablature and one part only provided for a third collection, *Musicalischer Andachten, Ander Theill* (Musical Devotions, Second Part).[69] In addition to the capellen, Mus. ms. 150 includes a score in organ tablature for sixty-four compositions from these three printed collections. These scores are intabulations of the original Hammerschmidt parts and do not include the capellen. Tables 1 and 2 in the appendix provide a list of Hammerschmidt's works, their additional capella parts, and describe the relationship between the prints and the Bohn collection.

The majority of the Bohn parts are designated for a voice and an instrument to share *colla parte*, as indicated with part titles such as "2 Cant[us] Voce è Cornett." Out of the fifty-two pieces in Ms. mus. 150 with both tablature and extant capella parts, only one—"Herr du weissest alle dinge"—adds just vocal parts, and no works call only for additional instruments. The most commonly found capella parts are for tenor voice and trombone (sixty-two parts), cantus voice and cornett (sixty-one), bass voice and either trombone or bombardo[70] (forty-nine), and altus voice and trombone (forty-four). Single parts designated for either one voice or one instrument only occur less frequently and normally double another part, suggesting that they were intended to facilitate performance by allowing performers to be placed in different locations. The number of Bohn parts added per piece ranges from two to fifteen, but the majority of works have four, five, or six added parts.

The most common ensembles that the Bohn parts provide as a complement to Hammerschmidt's original print are one or two cantus and cornett, along with two to four altus, tenor, and/or bassus voices, and trombones. Just three pieces add violins, and in two of these, the parts indicate that they may be replaced or doubled by the cornett. The trombone is added to all but three of the pieces, though the original print already called for trombones in two of these works. The cornett, if not found in the original print, has been added to all but five.

There are four different relationships between the capella parts and Hammerschmidt's original parts. The first type, which constitutes the majority of capella parts, includes those that strictly double parts in the original print: vocal parts with text have been added to what were originally instrumental parts, and instrumental parts double what were originally vocal parts.[71] The second type doubles original parts, but with minor alterations such as octave displacement or doubling, slight rhythmic simplification, added rests, or reiteration to follow the word setting. The third type consists of parts that are newly composed,[72] while the fourth type includes both sections that double original parts and sections that are newly composed.

Depending on how Hammerschmidt deployed the tutti in his works, the added capellen function to enhance the pieces of the original print in one of three ways.[73] In the first function, the capella complements the tuttis throughout the entire piece (thirty-one works). Second, the capella appears only with the final tutti (fourteen). Third, the capella reinforces the tuttis found throughout the final section or second half of the work (seven). When tuttis appear more than once, they function as a refrain about a third of the time. The compositions selected for this edition demonstrate both the structural enhancement these capellen provide and the various types of added Bohn parts.

Since the Bohn parts of Ms. mus. 150 do not duplicate complete pieces, but usually only tuttis, it is possible that the works in this edition were performed in two divided choirs, one of favoriten, consisting of solo vocalists and instrumentalists singing and playing from the Hammerschmidt prints, the other of capellen, with singers and instrumentalists performing *colla parte* from the Bohn parts. Two continuo keyboards could perform using the two partbooks and/or the tablature, although the latter may have been a conducting score. Even though the architecture of St. Maria Magdalena allowed for the positioning of as many as four choirs around the interior, only "Herr kom hinab" has enough of these separate duplicate parts to create a possible third choir.[74] Moreover, it also has an extra tablature part and an instrumental sinfonia to be added to the beginning, exemplifying Büttner's two other arrangement techniques mentioned above: composing instrumental preludes and turning pieces into polychoral works.[75]

Although it is not clear whether Hammerschmidt's music was ever performed with the supplementary parts, the music of Ms. mus. 150—indeed, the entire Bohn collection—tells us much about the vibrancy of the musical life, and especially the performance of sacred music, in seventeenth-century Breslau. It is clear that the addition of capellen described by Hammerschmidt, following the models established by both Praetorius and Schütz, was practiced in Breslau after 1656. It is also apparent that voices and instruments played *colla parte*, there was a tradition of using brass instruments in sacred music, and cornett and trombone players were available.[76] Finally, the fact that so many of Hammerschmidt's pieces were provided with capellen demonstrates the popularity and respect he enjoyed in this city.

The Music of the Edition

Freue dich, du Tochter Zion

Hammerschmidt inaugurated the liturgical year with "Freue dich, du Tochter Zion" (Rejoice, daughter of Zion), a joyful setting for the first Sunday of Advent scored for CCATB, two cornetins (cornettinos) or violins, and continuo. The non-conversational text is based principally on the gospel reading of the day (Matt. 21:1–9), which tells the story of Christ entering Jerusalem on a donkey (see the "Texts and Translations" for details concerning textual sources). Instead of beginning the work directly with the Gospel text, Hammerschmidt used a line from Zechariah 9:9 ("Rejoice, daughter of Zion"), to which Jesus refers in Matthew 21:5 ("Tell the daughter of Zion"). Indeed, the more militant verses surrounding the passage from Zechariah, which Luther called "warlike talk," may have inspired the vigor and energy in this work, as well as the use of cornetin.[77] While the text itself lacks dialogue, Hammerschmidt created a musical conversation through contrasts between soloists, instruments, and chorus. The tenor is the principal solo voice, which alternates with sections featuring solo bassus, cantus duet, cornetin duet, or combinations of the three. The Bohn capella parts are for CAATB doubled *colla parte* by cornett and four trombones, and they appear as a tutti throughout the piece. A sense of refrain-like unity is established with each utterance of the capella, which functions cadentially to close sections and highlight the most important words of praise to splendid effect.

Mein Sohn, warumb hast du uns das gethan?

Hammerschmidt's setting of Luke 2:48–49, "Mein Sohn, warumb hast du uns das gethan?" (My son, why have you done this to us?), the gospel for the first Sunday after Epiphany, uses three solo voices to depict the dialogue between the young Christ (altus) and his parents Mary (cantus) and Joseph (bassus), who have just found their child in the temple.[78] This work is especially unusual in that it is the only one in the 1655 collection scored for four strings (three violins and one violone) and clavicembalo, with the clavicembalo and violone creating a second continuo group whenever the strings are present.[79] Hammerschmidt employed a number of musical devices to underscore the relationship between Christ and God and between Christ and his parents. The music sung by Mary and Joseph at the work's opening is based on the interval of a descending third, which is first filled in stepwise (mm. 4–5), and later presented as an open third that is often expanded to a triad (mm. 6–8). These motives are frequently embellished and developed through sequence, imitation, combination, and contrapuntal inversion; these varied settings emphasize Mary and Joseph's insistent questioning and their struggle to understand the situation. Christ enters singing the motives of Mary and Joseph (mm. 23–27), but he then abandons this music—and, symbolically, his parents—with a different reiterative melodic line, joined by the strings and clavicembalo with the words "in dem das meines Vaters ist" (in that which is the house of my father). Indeed, his is the only voice to receive instrumental accompaniment, and the regal effect produced by the supporting instruments highlights his true heritage as the son of God. The separate continuo group, moreover, appears whenever Christ sings, further establishing his independence. The seven parts of the Bohn capella appear only to complement the tutti in the final section, the "Alleluja."

Herr, ich bin nicht werth

A setting for the third Sunday after Epiphany, "Herr, ich bin nicht werth" (Lord, I am not worthy) recounts the story from Matthew 8 of the centurion who believes that Christ's word alone can heal him and does not feel worthy enough to invite Christ to his house. Hammerschmidt's setting includes a number of elements associated with sacred dialogues discussed above: conversation, personification, and the use of repetition as practiced in meditation. The centurion's words are set for both solo tenor and cantus duet, each accompanied by continuo.[80] Notable is Hammerschmidt's integration of a trombone duet into the texture. These instruments make their first appearance in the opening sinfonia, and their rhythm is taken over by the tenor in his first entrance. Similar to the violins in "Mein Sohn, warumb hast du uns das gethan?" the trombone duet supports and echoes the words of Christ (bassus). In measure 53, the bassus introduces a motive of a descending and ascending minor second on "sey getrost" (have faith), which is in turn echoed and repeated by the trombones. By measure 71, the trombones present the motive independent of the voice, thus continuing to instill in the absence of text the message to have faith. The seven capella parts are added in the two sections of "Lobe den Herren" that occur in the last third of the piece.

O Herr hilf, wir verderben!

"O Herr hilf, wir verderben!" (O Lord save us, we are perishing!) sets an episode from Matthew 8:25–27, the gospel reading for the fourth Sunday after Epiphany.[81] Hammerschmidt's original ensemble (CCAATB plus continuo) lacks obbligato instruments, and the Bohn parts not only reinforce the chorus of favoriten throughout the piece but also demonstrate how instruments could be added to what was originally a purely vocal work. Structurally, the capella draws attention to significant phrases in alternation with vocal soloists and provides strong cadences at the end of sections.

The piece is divided musically and dramatically into three parts. In part 1 (mm. 1–70), the disciples (two cantus, altus, tenor, and the first bassus, all of whom are reinforced by the capella) call out to Christ (second bassus) for help as their boat is tossed in the stormy sea, and Christ admonishes them for their lack of faith. The opening line returns emphatically several times throughout this first part, functioning as a refrain until the cadential section that brings the first part to a close. These repetitious cries may have been inspired by Luther's sermon on this pericope, whereby Christ wants the Christian to cry out to him continually so that the believer can be saved repeatedly.[82] The chorus of favoriten (and added capellen) takes on other phrases in the rest of the work in the same manner. Part 2 (mm. 71–96) depicts Christ stilling the waters and the wonderment of the disciples; word painting occurs on "Wind und Meer" (wind and sea), which is set to two pairs of eighth notes (mm. 79–95). Part 3 (mm. 97–116) closes the work with a triple-meter "Alleluja." The exuberant entries of the favoriten throughout (representing the fear and awe of the disciples), the persistent and triumphant triadic solos of the second bassus, and the playful final "Alleluja" complement the liturgical day.[83]

"O Herr hilf, wir verderben!" incorporates a number of features of sacred dialogues: conversation, personification of a person and a group, and the use of timbral contrast. Hammerschmidt's original already creates a sense of polychoral drama through the division between the second bassus and the other favoriten, and the added capella parts accentuate this division and offer another level of contrast with all the favoriten. One unusual feature of the capella is a vocal part that is a composite of the most important melodies of the original tenor and two bassus parts. Composite parts like this occur in four other pieces in Ms. mus. 150. If one singer were capable of singing all these parts, he either strengthened the most important solo vocal phrases or replaced those voices in this condensed version. This part has not been transcribed in the present edition, but it appears as plate 3.

O Vater, aller Augen warten auff dich

In this Lenten piece for Laetare (the fourth Sunday of Lent), Hammerschmidt created a dialogue by combining two different biblical texts. A cantus duet sings repeatedly sections of Psalm 145, which praise God and reveal the desperate need of the people of Israel for guidance ("O Father, the eyes of all look to you"). In two places (measures 67 and 72), Hammerschmidt musically depicts the emptiness of the Christian's life without God: the bass line—representing the constant support of God—drops out for three beats before the cantus duet sings "du sättigest alles, was da lebet" (you satisfy the desire of every living thing), leaving only the right hand to realize the continuo figures. The bassus sings some of the commandments that God gave to Moses on Mount Sinai (Lev. 26:3–5). The reiteration of text demonstrates the repetitive aspect of meditation and pedagogy noted above. The choice of text is unusual in that it is not drawn from the gospel of the day (John 6:1–15). However, the words from Leviticus are related to the Gospel story of Christ feeding the multitudes with five loaves and two fish; both texts state that the Lord will provide for those who follow his laws.

In addition to the cantus duet and bassus, Hammerschmidt's setting features a trombone duet that not only provides two symphonias, but also echoes and emphasizes solo vocal and choral phrases. The trombone symphonias combine homophony with imitative technical sections. Unlike their role in "Herr, ich bin nicht werth," the trombones do not echo just the solo voice, but also the cantus duet, emphasizing their phrases with passages that include sixteenth notes requiring rapid tonguing. The rhythmic motive introduced by the bassus in measures 76–77 on "Werdet ihr meine Gebothe halten" (If you keep my commandments) is echoed by the trombones and reiterated by them when the bassus sings the rest of the phrase, thus continuing to emphasize that one should keep God's commandments. The trombono grosso of the capella (see plate 4) functions as a third trombone to the original trombone duet, creating a rich harmonic foundation.

The eight parts of the capella enter for the many tuttis found during the last third of the piece, which commences with a change to triple meter and the words "Dancket dem Herren" (Give thanks to the Lord, Ps. 106:1). This addition of the capella, as well as the line from Psalm 106, summarize much of what happened earlier in the work—thus functioning much like the *subscriptio* of an emblem as discussed above. Frequently giving thanks to God is an essential part of being Christian, and here the chorus, drawing the congregation in as tacit participant, praises God for doing so much for humanity while asking for little in return.

Gott fähret auff mit Jauchtzen!

This exuberant celebration of Ascension Sunday features two clarinos (or trombettas), two trombones, CCATB, and continuo supplemented by a capella of CATB, each *colla parte* with a cornett or trombone. The work is similar to "Freue dich, du Tochter Zion" in three ways: the only element of dialogue is the musical contrast between soloists, instruments, and chorus; the mood is festive; and the text is not from the Gospel. Instead, the text from Psalm 47:1–6 provides a poetic description of the Ascension that is found in neither the epistle (Acts 1:1–11) nor the gospel of the day (Mark 16:14–20).

Both *colla parte* playing and doubling between the favoriten and capellen give this work a rich texture and regal sound. The trombone parts of Hammerschmidt's setting are *colla parte* with the altus and tenor, perhaps serving as a model for the capella parts in Ms. mus. 150. The Bohn parts mostly double their respective vocal parts in the favoriten; in much the same fashion as in "O Vater, aller Augen warten auff dich," the trombono grosso serves as third trombone to the pair in the original print. The capella reappears throughout this piece, providing a concluding cadence to almost every section. The composition abounds in motives featuring triads, thirds, reiterations, and fanfares in both homophonic and imitative textures. These motives take as their inspiration idiomatic clarino technique: all the parts at one time or another perform trumpet fanfares that announce Christ's Ascension.

Vater Abraham

The pericope for the first Sunday after Trinity (Luke 16:19–31) tells the story of the rich man and poor Lazarus.[84] While Lazarus suffered during his lifetime, after his death he is "carried by the angels to Abraham's bosom" (Luke 16:22). The rich man goes to hell, where he sees Abraham and Lazarus in the distance and calls to Abraham to send Lazarus to his aid. Hammerschmidt set only verses 24–31, the dramatic dialogue between the rich man (altus) and Abraham (bassus).[85] The voices are accompanied by continuo and string choir (three violins, viola, and violone); unlike other works with a five-part string choir, this piece lacks a part for clavicembalo.

The string symphonia sets the tone with a fanfare-like opening in which the strings ascend a C major triad, perhaps depicting Lazarus's entry into heaven. The altus is usually accompanied only by the continuo, and his opening lines introduce several melodic motives that unify the composition. Particularly noticeable is the line "denn ich leide Pein" (for I am in agony), which introduces a sequence that includes a chromatically ascending fourth, illustrating the rich man's suffering. The strings fill in and sometimes echo the phrases of the bassus throughout the work.

Scored for CCATB, with trombone and bombardo playing *colla parte* with the tenor and bassus, the capella heightens the drama with varied timbres and increased volume. While Hammerschmidt's setting calls for only two voices—those of the rich man and Abraham—the capella joins the three violins and violone to echo and reinforce the words of Abraham, who states that the rich man's brothers must listen to Moses and the prophets if they wish to avoid hell. (Here is an instance of a vocal choir created from instrumental parts, the inverse of "O Herr hilf, wir verderben!" The music of the strings follows the rhythms of the bassus so closely that few modifications were needed for the text underlay to fit.) The capella also joins the bassus on the final line in an emphatic homophonic statement declaring that, if the brothers do not heed Moses and the prophets, they will never be convinced of the error of their ways—even if someone returns from the dead to warn them. This forceful sound is pitted against the single voice of the rich man, still uttering repeatedly "embarme dich mein" (have mercy on me); the entire altus part carries a sense of hopeless suffering and desperation, reflecting the rich man's predicament in hell. This repetition serves as a reminder to the congregation of what could befall them if they do not heed the prophets.

Es wird eine grosse Trübsal seyn

Hammerschmidt's setting for the twenty-fifth Sunday after Trinity brings together two related texts that deal with the day of judgment: Matthew 24:21–22 ("There will be great tribulation, such has not been") and the seventh verse of the chorale "Es ist gewisslich an der Zeit" by Bartholomäus Ringwald.[86] Like "O Vater, aller Augen warten auff dich," the dialogue of "Es wird eine grosse Trübsal seyn" results from the juxtaposition of two different texts and does not depict a conversation between two characters. The bassus sings the Gospel verses and is always accompanied by pairs of recorders and/or trombones, which also echo and respond to the voice's phrases. This particular instrumentation is unusual for Hammerschmidt's *Gespräche*; only one other piece includes the recorder, namely "So euch die Welt hasset" (1655).[87] The chorale text, "O Jesu Christ," is sung primarily by a cantus duet[88] and appears in alternation with the lines from the Gospel, sung by the bassus. The final section, marked "Ripieno" in the print, presents the chorale verse one last time and without interruption, but Hammerschmidt gives it a different melody; here, the third and fourth cantus, altus, and tenor voices sing *colla parte* with the recorders and trombones of the favoriten and are joined by the four capella parts.[89] The fullness of the harmonization and timbre of the homophonic chorale at the end brings comfort to the listeners, who realize that they are not alone in facing judgment day.

Notes on Performance

Instrumentation

Hammerschmidt supplied two figured partbooks for the continuo: one labeled "Violon *Nach Beliebung*," the other "Continuus," thus implying that the bass line was to be doubled. The organ is the obvious choice for the chordal continuo instrument in sacred music, and the organ tablature found in Ms. mus. 150 further supports this recommendation. As Hammerschmidt seems to have had timbral contrast in mind when calling for a harpsichord (abbreviated in the source as "Clavicimb," or clavicembalo) in those works with two separate continuo groups, another keyboard or chordal instrument (such as a regal) could be used as well, so long as its tone color is different from an organ. Advice for figured bass realization and organ registration is readily available elsewhere.[90]

Modern instruments may substitute for the stringed instruments named in the collections (violin, viola, and violone), including the modern violoncello for the violone. Hammerschmidt named the violin as a replacement for the cornetin. The only modern instrument that comes close to producing the sound of a cornett is the modern oboe, though a violin or any other treble woodwind instrument may serve just as well. The modern trumpet may substitute for clarino or trombetta (baroque straight trumpet). *Flauto* in German refers to a recorder in this period, although a modern flute could also be used in performance, particularly on the lower part.[91] Although Hammerschmidt used only the term "trombona," the three names for trombone found in the added Bohn parts seem to indicate different roles for the instrument: the trombin doubles the altus, the trombono the tenor, and the trombono grosso (or simply trombono) the bassus. According to Praetorius, an alto trombone is used when the uppermost notes are higher than a', which is rare in this repertoire.[92] The trombono grosso (also called "trombon grando" or "trombone majore" by Praetorius) is pitched a fourth or fifth below a tenor trombone, an octave below an alto.[93] Despite these different nomenclatures, a modern tenor trombone (or one with an F attachment) can be used on all parts. However, the modern trombone has a much larger bore than the instrument of the period and will probably be too loud for most ensembles and performing spaces. If sackbuts are unavailable, small-bore trombones should be used on all the upper parts, and a tenor trombone with an F attachment for the lowest part. The bombardo (bass shawm) may be replaced by a bassoon, trombone, violone, or any other fundamental bass instrument.

The Capella

Hammerschmidt offered the following suggestions for the placement of the favoriten and capellen in his *Vierdter Theil Musicalischer Andachten*:

The *concertato* voices and *favoriten* can be somewhat separated from the *capellen*, such that each is placed with discretion—but not too far apart, as is often the case. One will also be sure to pay attention to the advantages of the venue, and especially strive not to cause a silent devotion [in which the words are indistinguishable], but rather [to ensure] that above all the text be clearly and plainly pronounced and heard. Accordingly, a few prominent positions in the middle of the church near a regal should be chosen, depending on the characteristics of the song, so that the words may be better heard.[94]

Clearly, the acoustics of the performance space and the intelligibility of the text were foremost in Hammerschmidt's mind. He was also flexible about the inclusion of instruments, stating that "the added symphonies and instruments may be omitted. However, where instruments are available, they may reinforce the *Capella*."[95] In the second part of his *Musicalische Andachten*, Hammerschmidt further stated that he would "leave it to [the director's] discretion to conduct and employ at best either voices or instruments as the opportunity may present itself."[96] Hammerschmidt's remarks confirm that it was common practice to give the musical director some freedom in adding capellen to the tuttis of sacred works.

Articulation, Tempo, Pronunciation, and Ornamentation

In the first part of his *Musicalische Andachten*, Hammerschmidt opined that vocal and instrumental styles "[are] similar . . . thus in my little study I would try to compose for them both in the same [style]." [97] Since instruments often imitate motives first presented by the voices, the instruments need to "speak" like the singers. Hammerschmidt also emphasized the importance of enunciation on the part of the vocalists. In the instructions to the fourth part of his *Musicalische Andachten*, Hammerschmidt observed that "concertos are very praiseworthy, not only because the text can be better understood with a singer who pronounces it directly and correctly, but also because their charm usually evokes a remarkable devotion in the listeners." [98] To achieve this clarity of expression, Hammerschmidt recommended that a slower tempo be taken.[99] Similarly, the preface to the *Musicalische Gespräche* admonishes performers "to try to use a slow beat."[100] In the corrections provided after the table of contents to the *Musicalische Gespräche* (see "Sources" in the critical report), Hammerschmidt also stated that C was to replace all instances of ¢, a revision that again emphasizes the slower tempo. Tilley has written an excellent comparative summary of old and new spellings and their bearing on pronunciation.[101]

Hammerschmidt strictly forbade ornamentation, apparently as a result of hearing much misuse of embellishment. He declared in his preface to the *Musicalische Gespräche*:

> And I especially wish also, that those singers and instrumentalists who up to now are accustomed to use various vulgar and odd coloraturas, especially at the final [cadence], would be so kind as not to make this work of mine unacceptable with that sort of *Quintelirien* or so-called coloration, which sometimes sounds to the listener like the buzzing of flies, thereby thwarting themselves; but on the contrary, that they would leave the notes as they have been composed by me. The same applies also to singers and instrumentalists where it is appropriate to ornament with a charming trill. For those practiced and experienced musicians, however, I will not have to dictate the least instruction.[102]

Organ Tablature

All of the pieces found in Ms. mus. 150 have been intabulated into German organ tablature, and these tablatures are compiled into a single bound manuscript (see "Sources" in the critical report). It was not unusual in the sixteenth or seventeenth centuries to find German intabulations of complete vocal editions, though intabulations of miscellaneous compositions were more prevalent.[103] Although volumes of intabulations tended to include collections of a variety of composers and mingle sacred and secular genres, Johannes Rühling and Jacob Paix each published a tablature of purely sacred music, and Johann Woltz included a liturgical cycle in his printed tablature.[104] Intabulations of vocal pieces functioned as miniature scores for the organist, who was more often than not also the director of the church choir.[105] The tablature then served as a rehearsal score that took up little space, provided all the notes, and enabled the organist to read the music at a glance.[106] Andreas Werckmeister confirms this practice in *Musicalische Paradoxal Discourse* (1707):

> I have known various *directors* who wrote their scores in German *tablature* and sang and *directed* from them. Moreover, I can prove on the basis of the distinguished *Grimm's* own handwriting that he *conducted* from German *tablature*, or letter notation.[107]

Many German organists preferred to reduce scores themselves rather than read figures, and tablature allowed them to replace a choir in performance if necessary.[108] Exact intabulation was preferred in these cases because the pieces were not arrangements for the organ. Even Bohn described the organ tablatures of Ms. mus. 150 as "Part[itur] in Tab[ulatur]," or "score in tablature."[109] In fact, a few of Hammerschmidt's pieces had already been intabulated into two manuscript collections before Büttner's intabulations.[110] The practice of having an organ substitute for a choir in a polychoral piece has also been documented in German compositions and treatises since the early seventeenth century.[111]

This edition provides a transcription of the original Hammerschmidt print and Bohn partbooks, not the tablature. Although the tablature is also derived from the print and was probably used as a score, partial text underlay is provided only for "Gott fähret auff mit Jauchtzen!" (see plates 5 and 6) and "Vater Abraham"; there is no mention of the inclusion of the capella in the tablature. In all probability, Büttner was more comfortable directing from organ tablature, following common German practice. The creation of so many intabulations testifies to Hammerschmidt's popularity in Breslau.

Appendix

The following two tables present the contents of Andreas Hammerschmidt, *Musicalische Gespräche über die Evangelia* (1655) and *Ander Theil Geistlicher Gespräche über die Evangelia* (1656) with their corresponding capella parts from the Bohn Collection. Titles are taken from the registers of Andreas Hammerschmidt's *Gespräche* and regularized with respect to capitalization and punctuation; designations that appear in the register, such as "à 4" and "8 voc." have also been regularized. (See plate 2 for the first page of the register of the *Musicalische Gespräche* [1655].) As the titles listed in the Bohn catalogue vary from the Hammerschmidt prints only in spelling and length, they have not been included in these tables.

Voice and instrument names have been standardized and abbreviated as follows: A = Altus; B = Bassus; B.c. = Basso continuo; Bom. = Bombardo; C = Cantus; Clno. = Clarino; Clav. = Clavicembalo; Comp. = Composite part; Ctin. = Cornetin/Cornettino; Ct. = Cornett/Cornetto; Fl. = Flauto; Tab. = Tablature; T = Tenor; Tbta. = Trombetta; Trb. = Trombona; Trbo. = Trombono; Trbo. gr. = Trombono grosso; Va. = Viola; Vn. = Violino; Vne. = Violone. A slash indicates that instrumentation varies between register and partbooks; the register's instrumentation is given first, followed by that of the partbook. Shared parts are designated "C & Ct." The continuo part in both of Hammerschmidt's publications is provided in two figured partbooks, one labeled "Violon *Nach Beliebung*," the other "Continuus"; these are listed collectively as "B.c."

Although tablature is not listed in the table, the Bohn collection includes organ tablature for all works in Ms. mus. 150; "Viel sind beruffen" and "O Jesu wir wissen, daß du" (Bohn nos. 45 and 48; see table 2) each have an additional copy of tablature included with the parts. Several works in the Bohn collection include only tablature. As it is unclear whether there were ever capella parts for these pieces, they are listed in the table as having "Tab. only; no extant parts." The indication "no parts," is used for works that are not listed in the Bohn catalog and which lack both tablature and capella parts.

The following fonts have been used to describe the relationship between the Bohn parts and the original print: plain font = doubles one part of original print; plain font underlined = doubles one part of original with minor alterations (such as transposition up or down an octave); **bold and italics** = newly composed; *italics* = some sections double original print; other sections newly composed. An asterisk indicates that a capella part doubles portions of more than one part of the original print.

The following system has been used to describe the relationship between the print and manuscript parts: 1 = capella appears in tuttis throughout the piece; 2 = capella appears in final tutti only; 3 = capella appears in tuttis throughout final section or second half of piece; U = relationship unknown.

Table 1

Contents of Andreas Hammerschmidt, *Musicalische Gespräche über die Evangelia* (1655) and Corresponding Capella Parts from the Bohn Collection

Print No.	Feast	Title	Print Parts	Bohn Parts	Bohn No.	Capella Function
1	First Sunday of Advent	Freue dich, du Tochter Zion *a 6*	CCTB, B.c. 2 Vn./Ctin.	C & Ct. ***A1 & Trb.*** ***A2 & Trb.*** *T & Trb.* B & Trbo.	1	1
2	Second Sunday of Advent	Himmel und Erden vergehen *a 5*	CCATB, B.c.	C1 & Ct. C2 & Ct. A & Trb. ***T & Trb.*** B & Bom.	2	1
3	Third Sunday of Advent	Da aber Johannes die Werck Christi hörete *a 5*	CCATB, B.c.	Ct.1 C & Vn./Ct. *A & Trb.* ***T1 & Trb.*** ***T2 & Trb.*** B & Bom.	3	1

xvi

TABLE 1 continued

Print No.	Feast	Title	Print Parts	Bohn Parts	Bohn No.	Capella Function
4	Fourth Sunday of Advent	Und diß ist das Zeugnüß Johannis *a 5*	CCATB, B.c.	C1 & Ct. C2 & Vn./Ct. *A* T1 & Trb. *T2* B & Trbo.	4	2
5	The Nativity of Our Lord	O ihr lieben Hirten, fürchtet euch nicht *a 6*	CATB, B.c. 2 Vn./Ctin.	C & Ct.* A & Trb. T & Trb. B & Trb.	5	1
6	Sunday within the Octave of Christmas	Was meinestu wil aus dem Kindlein werden *a 5*	ATB, B.c. 2 Vn./Ctin.	*C1 & Ct.* *C2 & Ct.* A & Trb. T1 & Trb. T2 & Trb. B & Trbo.	6	2
7	The Circumcision of Our Lord	Und da acht Tage umb wahren *a 7*	CCATB, B.c. 2 Vn.	C & Ct. A & Trb. T & Trb. B & Bom.	7	1
8	The Epiphany of Our Lord	Wo ist der neugebohrne König der Jüden *a 7*	CCATB, B.c. 2 Vn.	C & Ct. A & Trb. T1 & Trb. *T2 & Trb.* B & Bom.	8	1
9	First Sunday after Epiphany	Mein Sohn, warumb hast du uns das gethan *a 7*	CAB, B.c. 3 Vn., Vne. & Clav.	C1 & Ct. C2 & Ct. *A & Trb.* T1 & Trb. Trb. *T2 & Trb.* B & Trbo.	9	2
10	Second Sunday after Epiphany	Herr sie haben nicht Wein *a 6*	CCTB, B.c. 2 Vn.	C1TB (Comp.) C1 C1 & Ct. C2 & Ct. A1 A2 & Trb. T B	10	2
11	Third Sunday after Epiphany	Herr ich bin nicht werth *a 6*	CCTB, B.c. 2 Trb.	C1 & Ct. C2 & Ct. Ct.2 A & Trb. T1 & Trb. T2 & Trb. B2 & Bom.	11	3
12	Fourth Sunday after Epiphany	O Herr hilf, wir verderben *a 6*	CCATBB, B.c.	C1 & Ct. C2 & Ct. Ct.2 A & Trb. TB1B2 (Comp.) T1 & Trb. *T2 & Trb.* B2 & Bom.*	12	1

TABLE 1 continued

Print No.	Feast	Title	Print Parts	Bohn Parts	Bohn No.	Capella Function
13	Fifth Sunday after Epiphany	Herr hastu nicht guten Saamen *a 5*	CCB, B.c. 2 Vn.	<u>C1 & Ct.</u> C2 & Ct. *A & Trb.* <u>T1 & Trb.</u> T2 & Trb. B & Trbo. gr.	13	2
14	Septuagesima Sunday	Herr, diese letzten haben nur eine Stunde gearbeitet *a 5*	CCB, B.c. 2 Vn.	C1 & Ct. C2 & Ct. *A & Trb.* <u>T1 & Trb.</u> T2 & Trb. B & Trbo.	14	2
15	Sexagesima Sunday	Höret zu es gieng ein Seeman aus zuseen *a 6*	CATB, B.c. 2 Vn.	*C1 & Ct.* *C2 & Ct.* A & Trb. T1 & Trb. *T2 & Trb.* <u>B & Bom.</u>	15	1
16	Quinquagesima Sunday (Esto mihi)	Gelobet sey der Herr *a 4*	AB, B.c. 2 Vn./Ctin.	*C1 & Ct.* <u>C2 & Ct.</u> A & Trb. *T & Trb.* B1 & Trb. B2 & Trbo.	16	1
17	First Sunday of Lent (Invocavit)	Bistu Gottes Sohn *a 4*	CCAB, B.c.	Tab. only; no extant parts	17	U
18	Second Sunday of Lent (Reminiscere)	Ach Herr, du Sohn David *a 4*	CATB, B.c.	*C1 & Ct.* *C2 & Ct.* A <u>T & Trb.</u> B1 & Trb. <u>B2 & Trbo.</u>	18	2
19	Third Sunday of Lent (Oculi)	O Jesu, mein Jesu *a 5*	CAB, B.c. 2 Trb.	*Ct.1* Ct.2 C & Ct. <u>A & Trb.</u> <u>T & Trb.</u> B & Trbo.*	56	2
20	Fourth Sunday of Lent (Laetare)	O Vater, aller Augen warten auff dich *a 5*	CCB, B.c. 2 Trb.	C1 & Ct. C2 & Ct. Ct.1 Ct.2 <u>A1 & Trb.</u> *A2 & Trb.* *T & Trb.* B & Trbo. gr.	53	3
21	Palm Sunday (Judica)	Wer von Gott ist *a 5*	CCB, B.c. 2 Trb.	No parts	—	—
22	Easter Sunday	Wer waltzet uns den Stein *a 7*	CCATB, B.c. 2 Vn.	C & Ct. A & Trb. *T & Trb.* <u>B & Trbo.</u>	54	3

TABLE 1 continued

Print No.	Feast	Title	Print Parts	Bohn Parts	Bohn No.	Capella Function
23	Low Sunday (Quasimodogeniti)	Friede sey mit euch *a 6*	CCTB, B.c. 2 Vn.	C2 & Ct. *A1* *A2 & Trb.* T & Trb. B & Trbo. Trb.	55	1
24	Second Sunday after Easter (Misericordias)	Ich bin ein guter Hirte *a 5*	CCB, B.c. 2 Trb.	Tab only; no extant parts	23	U
25	Third Sunday after Easter (Jubilate)	Warlich ich sage euch *a 5*	CCB, B.c. 2 Vn.	No parts	—	—
26	Fourth Sunday after Easter (Cantate)	Nun aber gehe ich hin *a 6*	CCAB, B.c. 2 Vn.	Tab only; no extant parts	19	U
27	Fifth Sunday after Easter (Rogate)	Warlich, ich sage euch, so ihr *a 7*	CCCTB, B.c. 2 Vn./Ctin.	*A & Trb.* *T & Trb.* B & Trbo. gr.	20	1
28	Ascension Day	Gott fähret auff mit Jauchtzen *a 7*	CCATB, B.c. 2 Clar./Tbta. 2 Trb.	C & Ctto A & Trb. T & Trb. B & Trbo. gr.*	21	1
29	Sixth Sunday after Easter (Exaudi)	So euch die Welt hasset *a 7*	CCATB, B.c. 2 Fl.	A & Trb. T & Trb. B & Bom.*	22	1
30	Pentecost	Herr, du weissest alle Dinge *a 7*	CCATB, B.c. 2 Vn.	A T B	52	1

TABLE 2

Contents of Andreas Hammerschmidt, *Ander Theil Geistlicher Gespräche über die Evangelia* (1656) and Corresponding Capella Parts from the Bohn Collection

Print No.	Feast	Title	Print Parts	Bohn Parts	Bohn No.	Capella Function
1	Trinity Sunday	Heilig ist der Herr *a 7*	CCATB, B.c. 2 Ctin.	C* A & Trb. T & Trb. B & Bom.	24	1
2	First Sunday after Trinity	Vater Abraham *a 7*	AB, B.c. 3 Vn.,[1] Va., Vne.[2]	C1 C2 A T & Trb. B & Bom.	25	2
3	Second Sunday after Trinity	Kommet denn es ist alles bereit *a 7*	CCATB, B.c. 2 Vn.	CAT (Comp.) A & Trb. T & Trb. B & Bom.	26	2
4	Third Sunday after Trinity	Freuet euch mit mir *a 8*	CTB, B.c. 3 Vn., Va., Vne. & Clav.[2]	C1 C2 & Ct. A T1 & Trb. T2 B	27	1

TABLE 2 continued

Print No.	Feast	Title	Print Parts	Bohn Parts	Bohn No.	Capella Function
5	Fourth Sunday after Trinity	Seyd barmhertzig *a 6*	CCT, B.c. 3 Trb.	CT (Comp.) C Ct.1 Ct.2 A1 A2 & Trb. T & Trb. B	28	3
6	The Nativity of John the Baptist	Gelobet sey der Herr *a 7*	CCATB, B.c. 2 Ctin.	*C & Ct.* A & Trb. T & Trb. B & Trbo.	29	1
7	The Visitation of the Virgin Mary	Meine Seele erhebet *a 7*	CCATB, B.c. 2 Ctin.	A & Trb. T & Trb. B & Trbo.	30	1
8	Fifth Sunday after Trinity	Simon fahre auf die Höhe *a 5*	ATB, B.c. 2 Vn.	*C1 & Ct.* <u>C2 & Ct.</u> A & Trb. T & Trb. B & Trbo. gr.	31	3
9	Sixth Sunday after Trinity	Wer mit seinem Bruder zürnet *a 6*	CCT, B.c. 3 Trb.	C1 & Ct. C2 & Ct. Ct. 2 A T B	32	1
10	Seventh Sunday after Trinity	Woher nehmen wir Brod *a 7*	CCATB, B.c. 2 Vn.	C & Ct. A & Trb. T1 & Trb. *T2 & Trb.* B & Bom.	40	1
11	Eighth Sunday after Trinity	Seht euch für vor den falschen Proph[eten] *a 6*	CCAB, B.c. 2 Vn.	<u>C & Ct.</u> A & Trb. <u>T1</u> *T2 & Trb.* B & Trbo. gr.	33	1
12	Ninth Sunday after Trinity	Wie hör ich das von dir *a 6*	CCTB, B.c. 2 Va. di braccio	C1 & Ct. C2 & Ct. A T B & Trbo. gr.	34	2
13	Tenth Sunday after Trinity	Mein Hauß ist ein Bethhauß *a 7*	CCATB, B.c. 2 Ctin.	<u>C & Ct.</u> A & Trb. T & Trb. <u>B & Trbo. gr.</u>	35	1
14	Eleventh Sunday after Trinity	Ich dancke dir Gott daß *a 5*	ATB, B.c. 2 Vn.	*C & Ct.* A & Trb. *T & Trb.* <u>B & Trbo. gr.</u>	36	2
15	Twelfth Sunday after Trinity	O mein Jesu du hast alles wolgemacht *a 6*	AB, B.c. 2 Vn. 2 Trb.	C & Ct. A* *T & Trb.* <u>B & Trbo. gr.</u>	37	2

TABLE 2 continued

Print No.	Feast	Title	Print Parts	Bohn Parts	Bohn No.	Capella Function
16	Thirteenth Sunday after Trinity	Meister, waß muß ich thun *a 7*	CCATB, B.c. 2 Vn.	C & Ct. A & Trb. T & Trb. B & Trbo.	38	1
17	Fourteenth Sunday after Trinity	Jesu lieber Meister *a 7*	CCATB, B.c. 2 Vn. T & Trb. B & Trbo.	C & Ct.* A & Trb.	39	1
18	Fifteenth Sunday after Trinity	Woher nehmen wir Br[od] *a 7* (= no. 10)				
19	Sixteenth Sunday after Trinity	Jüngling, ich sage dir *a 7*	CCAB, B.c. 3 Trb.[3]	C1 & Ct. C2 & Ct.	42	1
20	Seventeenth Sunday after Trinity	Wer sich selbst erhöhet *a 5*	ATB, B.c. 2 Vn.	C1 & Ct. C2 & Ct. A & Trb. T & Trb. B & Bom.	43	1
21	Eighteenth Sunday after Trinity	Meister was muß ich [thun] *a 7* (= no. 16)				
22	Nineteenth Sunday after Trinity	Wende dich Herr *a 7*	AB, B.c. 2 Vn. 3 Trb.	C1 & Ct. C2 & Ct. A & Trb. T1 & Trb. *T2 & Trb.* B & Trbo.	44	3
23	Twentieth Sunday after Trinity	Viel sind beruffen *a 7*	CCATB, B.c. 2 Vn.	C & Ct. A & Trb. T1 & Trb. *T2 & Trb.* B & Bom.	45	1
24	Twenty-first Sunday after Trinity	Herr kom hinab *a 6*	CCTB, B.c. 2 Vn.	*A & Trb.* Trb. 1 T1 & Trb. *T2 & Trb.* Trb. 2 B2 & Bom. Trb. 3[4]	46	1
25	Twenty-second Sunday after Trinity	Du Schalcksknecht *a 7*	CB, B.c. 2 Ctin. 3 Trb.	C1 & Ct.* C2 & Ct.* A & Trb. T1 & Trb. *T2 & Trb.* B & Trbo.	47	3
26	Michaelmas	Und es erhub sich ein Streit *ab 8. voc.*[5]	CATB & 4 Tbta. CC & 2 Ct. 2 Clno./Tbta. B.c.	Ct. 1 Ct. 2 C2 & Ct.* A & Trb. *T1 & Trb.* T2 & Trb. B & Bom.	41	1

TABLE 2 continued

Print No.	Feast	Title	Print Parts	Bohn Parts	Bohn No.	Capella Function
27	Twenty-third Sunday after Trinity	O Jesu wir wissen, daß du *a 7*	CCATB, B.c. 2 Vn.	C1 & Ct.* C2 & Ct. A & Trb. T & Trb. B & Trbo. Trb. 1 *Trb. 2* Trbo. gr.	48	1
28	Twenty-fourth Sunday after Trinity	Ich bin die Auferstehung *a 6*	Voce sola [T], B.c. 3 Vn., Va., Vne. & Clav.²	Tab only; no extant parts	49	U
29	Twenty-fifth Sunday after Trinity	Es wird eine grosse Trübsal seyn *a 7*	CCB, B.c. 2 Fl. 2 Trb.	C & Ct. A & Trb. *T & Trb.* B & Trbo. gr.	50	2
30	Twenty-sixth Sunday after Trinity	Kommet her ihr geseegneten *a 10*	CCATB, B.c. 3 Vn., Va., Vne. & Clav.²	CT1 (comp) A T & Trb. B & Trbo.	51	1
31	Twenty-seventh Sunday after Trinity	Darum wachet, denn ihr wisset weder T[ag] *a 7*	CCATB, B.c. 2 Vn.	No parts	—	—

¹ First violin partbook lists cornetin on the title page and violin on the second page.
² The register names "5. Viol.," referring to three violins, viola, and violone in the parts.
³ Text is added to the trombone parts in tutti sections, implying that they were to be joined by an additional altus, tenor, and bassus.
⁴ The Bohn collection also includes an added sinfonia with newly-composed parts for two violins, three trombonas, and trombono grosso, as well as organ tablature.
⁵ The phrase "ab 8 voc." (from eight voices) in the register indicates several optional tutti doublings named in the partbooks: the four voices are doubled by four trombettas "im Trippel" (i.e., the tutti sections, all of which are in triple meter), the two cantus voices are doubled by cornetti, and the two continuus partbooks also list violone.

Notes

1. The *Musicalische Gespräche über die Evangelia* exemplifies the dissemination of one publication. Partbooks for this print are currently found in thirty-seven libraries in Austria, Belgium, England, Germany, the Netherlands, Poland, Romania, Russia, Sweden, Switzerland, and the United States. See "Sources" in the critical report. Even during his own lifetime, Hammerschmidt is named in inventories from Zwickau to Berlin and Lübeck to Helsingør, as well as in the Düben collection in Sweden. Jack W. Schmidt outlines these sources in "The 'Musicalische Andachten' of Andreas Hammerschmidt" (Ph.D. diss., Northwestern University, 1993), 22–23.

2. Schütz wrote a poem of commendation for Hammerschmidt's *Fünffter Theil Musicalischer Andachten* (1652–53). A translation may be found in John Brooks Howard, "The Latin Lutheran Mass of the Mid-Seventeenth Century: A Study of Andreas Hammerschmidt's *Missae* (1663) and Lutheran Traditions of Mass Composition" (Ph.D. diss., Bryn Mawr College, 1983), 34.

3. For more information on the reception of Hammerschmidt and his music, including English translations of eighteenth-century commentaries, see Schmidt, "Musicalische Andachten," 19–40; Howard, "The Latin Lutheran Mass of the Mid-Seventeenth Century," 42–86; and Jack W. Schmidt, "A Composer's Dilemma: Andreas Hammerschmidt and the Lutheran Theology of Music," *The Choral Journal* 40 (December 1999): 24–25. According to Kerala J. Snyder, Hammerschmidt was very popular in Denmark and was the most represented composer in the music library of St. Mary's in Lübeck. Kerala J. Snyder, *Dieterich Buxtehude: Organist in Lübeck*, rev. ed. (Rochester: University of Rochester Press, 2007), 18 and 96.

4. A succinct biography is provided in Janette Tilley, introduction to Andreas Hammerschmidt, *Geistlicher Dialogen Ander Theil*, Recent Researches in the Music of the Baroque Era, vol. 150 (Middleton, Wis.: A-R Editions, 2008), xi.

5. Fuhrmann named Hammerschmidt and his contemporary Johann Rosenmüller (ca. 1619–84) as composers who used

triple meter frequently. Hammerschmidt is also cited in Fuhrmann's definition of *Motetto seu Muteta*; Fuhrmann called this style the *Hammerschmiedischen Fuß*, defined as "a church harmony, four voices strong (sometimes more) without instruments, set according to Hammerschmidt's standard, in which the voices make fugues and concertize only a little or not at all." Martin Fuhrmann, *Musicalischer-Trichter: dadurch ein geschickter Informator seinen Informandis die edle Singe-Kunst nach heutiger Manier bald und leicht einbringen kan* (Frankfurt an der Spree [Berlin], 1706), 46 and 82; quoted and translated in Snyder, *Dieterich Buxtehude*, 150.

6. Walther's lexicon presents biographical data, a works list, and the inscription on Hammerschmidt's tombstone. Johann Walther, *Musicalisches Lexicon oder Musicalische Bibliothec* (Leipzig, 1732; repr., ed. Friederike Ramm, Kassel: Bärenreiter, 2001), 271.

7. Johann Beeren [Bähr], *Musicalische Discurse* (Nuremberg: Peter Conrad Monath, 1719), 72–73; quoted and translated in Schmidt, "A Composer's Dilemma," 25. An overview of Bähr's discussion of Hammerschmidt is provided in Schmidt, "Musicalische Andachten," 26–29.

8. For a list and survey of other liturgical cycles, see Harold Mueller, "The Musicalische Gespräche über die Evangelia of Andreas Hammerschmidt" (Ph.D. diss., University of Rochester, Eastman School of Music, 1956), 124.

9. Janette Marie Tilley, "Dialogue Techniques in Lutheran Sacred Music of Seventeenth-Century Germany" (Ph.D. diss., University of Toronto, 2003), 118–19. One example of an emblem cycle Tilley cites is Johann Dilherr and Georg Philipp Harsdörffer, *Drei-ständige Sonn- und Festtag-Emblemata, oder Sinne-bilder* (Nuremberg, 1660; repr., Hildesheim: Olms, 1994).

10. John W. Doberstein, "Introduction," *Sermons I*, vol. 51, *Luther's Works*, ed. Helmut T. Lehmann (Philadelphia: Fortress, 1959; electronic ed., *Luther's Works on CD-ROM*, ed. Jaroslav Pelikan and Helmut T. Lehmann [Minneapolis: Fortress and Concordia, Libronix Digital Library System, 2002]).

11. Hans J. Hillerbrand, "Introduction," *Sermons II*, vol. 52, *Luther's Works*, ed. Helmut T. Lehmann (Philadelphia: Fortress, 1974; electronic ed., *Luther's Works on CD-ROM*). Luther's *Postille* are found throughout *D. Martin Luthers Werke, Kritische Gesamtausgabe*, 120 vols. (Weimar: Hermann Böhlau, 1883–2009).

12. Music might also be performed after the epistle or during Communion. See Charlotte A. Leonard, introduction to *Seventeenth-Century Lutheran Church Music with Trombones*, Recent Researches in the Music of the Baroque Era, vol. 131 (Middleton, Wis.: A-R Editions, 2003), viii.

13. Rhau was certainly living in Wittenberg when the ninety-five theses were posted, and he produced other Lutheran publications. *The New Grove Dictionary of Music and Musicians*, 2nd ed. (hereafter *NG2*), s.v. "Rhau, Georg" (p. 255) by Victor H. Mattfeld. Rhau's *Officia* (1539), *Officiorum* (1545), and *Evangelia dominicorum et festorum* (1554) all contain motets of the Gospels for the principal feasts of the church year by various composers. See also *NG2*, s.v. "Lutheran Church Music, 2(ii)(d): Origins and Consolidation (1523–80): Hauptgottesdienst" (p. 372), by Robin A. Leaver.

14. Jonah Clarence Kliewer, "The German Sacred Dialogues of the Seventeenth Century" (D.M.A. diss., University of Southern California, 1970), 50. Another term is *Evangelienmotette*, described in *Die Musik in Geschichte und Gegenwart*, 2nd ed. (hereafter *MGG2*), Sachteil, s.v. "Evangelium B. Evangelisch III. Mehrstimmige Vertonungen" (col. 220), by Joachim Stalmann and Christhard Mahrenholz.

15. Raselius's *Teutscher Sprüche auss den sontäglichen Evangeliis durchs gantze Jar* (Nuremberg, 1594) is the first such Gospel motet cycle in German; motets are listed by liturgical day. *NG2*, s.v. "Raselius, Andreas" (p. 836), by Walter Blankenburg. See also Andreas Raselius, *Cantiones Sacrae*, ed. Ludwig Roselius, Denkmäler der Tonkunst in Bayern, vol. 36 (Wiesbaden: Breitkopf & Härtel, 1972), lvi–lviii. Johannes Wanning is credited as being "the first Protestant composer to write cycles of *de tempore* motets for the whole church year," and his Latin motets served as the model for collections of *Spruchmotetten* by Raselius and other German composers. *NG2*, s.v. "Wanning, Johannes" (p. 82), by Walter Blankenburg and Clytus Gottwald. Other sixteenth-century composers of Gospel motet cycles include Sethus Calvisius, Jacobus Handl, and Leonhard Paminger. Orlando di Lasso also published seventeen Gospel motets. See Leaver, "Lutheran Church Music."

16. Demantius was one of the leading musical figures in Freiberg for thirty-nine years, serving as cantor at the cathedral and city school. *NG2*, s.v. "Demantius, Christoph" (p. 190), by Walter Blankenburg and Dorothea Schröder. Hammerschmidt may have known Demantius's liturgical cycle based on the Gospel, entitled *Corona harmonica, ausserlesene Sprüch aus den Evangelien, auff alle Sontage und fürnembste Fest durch das gantze Jahr* (Leipzig: Abraham Lamberg, 1610). It contains sixty-nine pieces labeled according to liturgical function, with some titles matching those found in Hammerschmidt's *Gespräche*.

17. Hammerschmidt's other two dialogue publications are not liturgical cycles. *Dialogi, oder Gespräche zwischen Gott und einer gläubigen Seelen, erster Theil* (Dresden, 1645), contains twenty-two dialogues in two to four parts with continuo published as Andreas Hammerschmidt, *Dialogi, oder Gespräche einer gläubigen Seele mit Gott: erster Theil*, ed. Anton Wilhelm Schmidt, Denkmäler der Tonkunst in Österreich, vol. 16 (1901; repr., Graz: Akademische Druck- und Verlagsanstalt, 1959). *Geistlicher Dialogen Ander Theil* (Dresden, 1645) contains twelve dialogues that are settings of Martin Opitz's poetic paraphrase of the Song of Solomon for one or two voices, two violins, and continuo and is available in Tilley, *Geistlicher Dialogen*.

18. Ahle's *Erster Theil Geistlicher Dialogen deren Etliche aus denen durchs Jahr über gewöhnlichen Sonn- und Fest Tags Evangelien* (Erfurt, 1648) contains twenty dialogues, although specific liturgical designations are inconsistently provided. In contrast with Hammerschmidt's *Gespräche*, the pieces are small-scale works in two to four parts including continuo. For the list of contents see Markus Rathey, *Johann Rudolph Ahle, 1625–1673: Lebensweg und Schaffen* (Eisenach: Karl Dieter Wagner, 1999), 564–68. Tilley has named eight other dialogues by Ahle found in four of his other collections. Tilley, "Dialogue Techniques," 232.

19. Briegel published six cycles of dialogues, including three volumes of *Evangelische Gespräche* that cover the entire church year. Although both Hammerschmidt and Briegel were among the first to interpolate texts from other sources into their Gospel settings, Briegel tended to employ the rhymes and strophic structures of chorales. Wolfgang Carl Briegel, *Erster Theil Evangelischer Gespräch Auff die Sonn- und Hauptfestage von Advent bis Sexagesima* (Frankfurt: Thomas Matthias Gözen, printed in Mühlhausen, Johann Hüter, 1660); *Ander Theil Evangelischer Gespräch Auff die Sonn- und Haupt Festage von Quinquagesima bis Pfingsten* (Frankfurt: Thomas Matthias Gözen, printed in Mühlhausen, Johann Hüter, 1661 and 1662); and *Dritter und letzter Theil Evangelischer Gespräch Vom ersten Sontag Trinitatis an, biß auff den XXVI* (Darmstadt: Henning Müller, 1681). The other dialogue collections include *Musicalische Trostquelle, Auß den Gewöhnlichen Fest- und Sontagsevangelien auch andern Biblischen Sprüchen geleitet* (Darmstadt: Albrecht Ottho Faber, printed by Henning Müller, 1679), *Musicalischer Lebensbrunn . . . meistentheils Gesprächs-Weise eingerichtet* (Darmstadt: Albrecht Ottho Faber, printed by Henning Müller, 1680), and *Apostolische Chor-Music* (Gießen: Henning Müller, 1697). Nine other individual dialogues also exist. According to Tilley's account, Briegel composed 290 dialogues. Tilley, "Dialogue Techniques," 234–35.

20. *MGG2*, Sachteil, s.v. "Dialog" (cols. 1200–1201), by Werner Braun. Hammerschmidt's version of this Easter dialogue is found in the *Musicalische Gespräche* as *Wer waltzet uns den Stein*. A score is available in Mueller, "Musicalische Gespräche," 91–106.

21. For a detailed account of the term "dialogue" in modern musicology, see Tilley, "Dialogue Techniques," 1–24.

22. Michael Praetorius, *Syntagma musicum III*, trans. and ed. Jeffery T. Kite-Powell (New York: Oxford University Press, 2004), 31.

23. "*Dialogi:* seynd solche Gesänge da etliche stimmen/ andern auff beschehene Fragen/ Antwort geben ... *Echo* ist solcher Art/ wie ein *Dialogus,* ohn allein daß die *respondirenden* Stimmen/ den vorhergehenden zu end einer Frage/ mit etlichen Noten an *Harmoni* müssen gleich seyn/ doch gar *submißè, pian* oder still müssen gesungen werden." Christoph Demantius, *Isagoge artis musicae ad incipientium captum maxime accommodata: Kurtze Anleitung recht und leicht singen zu lernen* (Freiberg: Georg Beuther, 1656). The terms are listed in the appendix. Unless otherwise noted, all translations are by the author.

24. Johann Rudolph Ahle, *Brevis et perspicua introductio in artem musicam, das ist: Kurtze und doch deutliche Anleitung zu der lieblichen, loblichen und ewigwürenden Singekunst* (Mühlhausen: Johann Hutter, 1673). The term is listed in the index.

25. Johann Rudolf Ahle, *Kurze, doch deutliche Anleitung zu der lieblichen und löblichen Singekunst, vor vielen jahren verfasset, und etliche mahl herausgegeben von Johan Rudolf Ahlen,* 2nd. ed., ed. Johann Georg Ahle (Mühlhausen: Michael Keiser, printed by Tobias David Brükner, 1704), 29–30.

26. "*Echo,* ein Wiederhall/ solches macht *submisse* ein am verborgenen Ort gestelltes Chor." Fuhrmann, *Musicalischer-Trichter,* 82.

27. "Echo: when a choir answers the other from a distance, or the instruments imitate a quiet cadence." (Echo, ein Wiederschall/ wann ein Chor von weitem dem andern antwortet/ oder die *Instrumen*ten eine *Clausul subtil* nachmachen.) Daniel Speer, *Grund-richtiger, kurtz-, leicht- und nöthiger, jetzt wohlvermehrter Unterricht der musicalischen Kunst: oder vierfaches musicalisches Kleeblatt . . .* (Ulm: Georg Wilhelm Kühne, 1697), 285.

28. "[A] dialogue . . . is a composition of at least two voices, or as many instruments, that perform in alternation and form a trio with the thoroughbass when they join together at the end; but there are also compositions for 2, 3, and 4 choirs that alternate like in a conversation. Organists also imitate the same kind of exchanges on the organ if they have more than one manual." (*Dialogo . . .* ist eine *Composition* wenigstens von zwo Stimmen, oder so viel Instrumenten, so wechsels-weise sich hören lassen, und wenn sie am Ende zusammen kommen, mit dem *G. B.* ein *Trio* machen; es giebt aber auch *Compositiones* auf 2. 3. und 4 Chöre, so Gesprächs-weise *altnir*en. Die Organisten *imiti*ren dergleichen Umwechselungen auch auf den Orgeln, wenn sie mehr als ein Clavier haben.) Walther, *Musicalisches Lexicon,* 188.

29. Ernest C. Harriss, *Johann Mattheson's Der vollkommene Capellmeister: A Revised Translation with Critical Commentary* (Ann Arbor, Mich.: UMI Research Press, 1981), 444–45.

30. Tilley, "Dialogue Techniques," 45–46.

31. John Butt, *Music Education and the Art of Performance in the German Baroque* (Cambridge: Cambridge University Press, 1994), 8. Luther's approach to presenting the Ten Commandments in the small catechism, for example, is to state the commandment, ask the question "what does it mean?" and then state his answer. Martin Luther, "Enchiridion: The Small Catechism of Dr. Martin Luther for Ordinary Pastors and Preachers," in *The Book of Concord: The Confessions of the Evangelical Lutheran Church,* trans. and ed. Theodore G. Tappert (Philadelphia: Fortress Press, 1959), 342–44. In fact, the catechism has been cited as the source of the "Frage-Antwort-System" of pedagogy used in seventeenth-century elementary schools. This format, also called "Dialogform," was used to teach Latin, as demonstrated by the title of Andreas Reyher's text: *Dialogi seu Colloquia* or *Kindische Gespräch und Unterredungen/ . . . Welche zu dem ersten Cursu der Lateinischen Sprache anzuführen* (1653). Martin Petzolt, "Ut probus a doctus reddar: Zum Anteil der Theologie bei der Schulausbildung Johann Sebastian Bachs in Eisenach, Ohrdruf und Lüneburg," *Bach-Jahrbuch* 71 (1985): 19 and 37.

32. Doberstein, "Introduction."

33. Butt states that the question-and-answer format is used extensively in music treatises and refers specifically to its use in the writings of Heinrich Faber (*Compendiolum musicae pro incipientibus* [Brunswick, 1548]), Cyriacus Schneegass (*Deutsche Musica für die Kinder und andere, so nicht sonderlich Latein verstehen* [Erfurt, 1592]), and François de La Marche (*Synopsis musica* [Munich, 1656]). Butt, *Music Education and the Art of Performance,* 8, 9, 54, and 67. Faber's work, the most popular music textbook in Lutheran schools at the time, appeared in thirty editions over the course of the sixteenth and seventeenth centuries. *NG2,* s.v. "Faber, Heinrich" (p. 488), by Clement A. Miller. J. R. Ahle's *Singekunst,* which was designed to train schoolboys, similarly made use of the question-and-answer technique.

34. Thoinot Arbeau, *Orchesography,* trans. Mary Stewart Evans (New York: Dover, 1967).

35. In her extensive study on the subject, Tilley lists 104 prints and 100 dialogues in manuscript by 93 composers. Tilley, "Dialogue Techniques," 232–52.

36. Johann Rudolf Ahle, for example, was trained in theology at Erfurt University, where he would have studied rhetoric as part of his education. *NG2,* s.v. "Ahle, Johann Rudolf" (p. 242), by George G. Buelow.

37. According to Tilley, "most sacred musical dialogues reveal this modern seventeenth-century approach to rhetoric as a tool for emotional affect rather than direct instruction." Tilley, "Dialogue Techniques," 112. This conclusion is based on the popularity of the writings of Gerhard Johann Vossius (1577–1649), whose four works on rhetoric emphasized the emotional power of rhetoric and were highly influential in the period. See Thomas Conley, *Rhetoric in the European Tradition* (New York: Longman, 1990), 159–61.

38. Tilley has identified four kinds of personification in her study, whereby the following are given voice: 1) a dead character or person; 2) God, Jesus or the Holy Spirit; 3) a living person (i.e., grieving widow); and 4) an abstraction (i.e., the soul). See Tilley, "Dialogue Techniques," 47–114.

39. For a complete discussion of the place of personification within rhetoric as part of seventeenth-century education, see ibid., 47–55.

40. The reason for using the bass voice to represent the mature Christ, as is the case in all pieces in this edition, may also be pedagogical, allowing the congregation to recognize Christ's words through this vocal timbre. Leaver notes that Luther set Christ's words for the lowest voice in his *Deutsche Messe,* in order "to teach the attending congregation to listen for the words of Christ, always heard at the lower pitch." Robin A. Leaver, *Luther's Liturgical Music: Principles and Implications* (Grand Rapids, Mich.: William B. Eerdmans, 2007), 184 and 193.

41. For a fuller exposition of emblems and applied emblematics, see Tilley, "Dialogue Techniques," 115–71, esp. 116–19.

42. Ibid., 116.

43. Ibid., 136.

44. Albrecht Schöne, *Emblematik und Drama im Zeitalter des Barock* (Munich: C. H. Beck, 1964), 163–64; quoted and translated in Tilley, "Dialogue Techniques," 134. For more on the relationship between emblems, *Reyen,* and the tutti chorus of musical *Gespräche,* see ibid., 37–38 and 141.

45. Historians remain divided as to whether the cause of this increase in piety and meditation was socially or devotionally inspired. Social problems emanated from the Thirty Years' War, while other religious problems may have stemmed from the fact that many Lutherans felt that simply attending the sermon sufficiently fulfilled their Christian duty. Ibid., 173–75.

46. Johann Gerhard (1582–1637) was a leading writer on Lutheran dogma and private devotional practice whose works remained current into the nineteenth century. According to Udo Sträter, *Meditationes Sacrae* had appeared in twelve languages and in 115 editions by 1700. Udo Sträter, *Meditation und Kirchenreform in der lutherischen Kirche des 17. Jahrhunderts,* ed. Johannes Wallmann, Beiträge zur historischen Theologie 91 (Tübingen: J. C. B. Mohr, 1995), 43.

47. Martin Luther, *Career of the Reformer IV,* ed. Lewis W. Spitz, vol. 34, *Luther's Works,* ed. Helmut T. Lehmann (Philadelphia: Fortress, 1960; electronic ed., *Luther's Works on CD-ROM*). See also Tilley, "Dialogue Techniques," 179–81.

48. Ibid., 188–90.

49. For example, Bukofzer has stated that Hammerschmidt was "a most prolific and popular composer who watered down the achievements of Schütz for the multitude." Manfred Bukofzer, *Music in the Baroque Era: From Monteverdi to Bach* (New York: W. W. Norton, 1947), 87.

50. The cornetin is pitched a fifth higher than the cornett. See Michael Praetorius, *Syntagma musicum II: De Organographia Parts I and II*, trans. and ed. David Z. Crookes (Oxford: Clarendon, 1986), 47.

51. The other three are from the 1656 collection: "Heilig ist der Herr" is a setting of Isaiah 6:3 and verse 3 of the chorale "Es woll uns Gott genädig sein." "Wende dich Herr" is a setting of Psalm 25:16–17. "Und es erhub sich ein Streit" is based on the epistle of the day (Revelations 12:7–12) rather than the Gospel. Mueller discusses the texts of the twenty-one pieces he edited in "Musicalische Gespräche," 99–123.

52. For the list of the forty-two dialogues, see Michael Märker, *Die protestantische Dialogkomposition in Deutschland zwischen Heinrich Schütz und Johann Sebastian Bach: eine stilkritische Studie*, Kirchenmusikalische Studien 2 (Köln: Studio, 1995), 16–17.

53. The remaining four works are all from the 1656 collection: "Heilig ist der Herr," "Meine Seele erhebet," "Und es erhub sich ein Streit," and "Ich bin die Auferstehung."

54. Leonard, introduction to *Seventeenth-Century Lutheran Church Music*, xiii–xiv; and Charlotte A. Leonard, "Hammerschmidt's Representation in the Bohn Collection: the *Capella* Tradition in Practice," in *Early Music: Context and Ideas* (Krakow: Institute of Musicology, Jagiellonian University, 2003), 282–305. See also Harold E. Samuel, "Michael Praetorius on Concertato Style," in *Cantors at the Crossroads: Essays on Church Music in Honor of Walter E. Buszin*, ed. Johannes Reidel (St. Louis: Concordia, 1967), 97–99; Snyder, *Dieterich Buxtehude*, 364–65; Schmidt, "Musicalische Andachten," 117–19; and Fritz Koschinsky, "Das protestantische Kirchenorchester im 17. Jahrhundert, unter Berücksichtigung des Breslauer Kunstschaffens dieser Zeit" (Ph.D. diss., Schlesische Friedrich-Wilhelms-Universität zu Breslau, 1931).

55. Praetorius, *Syntagma musicum*, vol. 3, *Termini musici*, 196; quoted and translated in Snyder, *Dieterich Buxtehude*, 365.

56. Heinrich Schütz, *Psalmen Davids 1619*, ed. Wilhelm Ehmann, Neue Ausgabe sämtlicher Werke 25 (Kassel: Bärenreiter, 1981), xviii; quoted and translated in George J. Buelow, "A Schütz Reader: Documents on Performance Practice," *American Choral Review* 27 (1985): 8.

57. "*Capella*, ist erstlich ein sonderlicher Chor/ welcher zu gewisser Zeit in den *Clausulis*, gleich wie die *Ripieni*, zu Stärckung und Pracht der Music mit einfället." Johann Andreas Herbst, *Musica moderna prattica* (Frankfurt: Georg Müller, 1658), 75.

58. "Muß dahero an einem *a parten* Ort von den *Concert*isten abgesondert gestellt werden. Es können aber diese *Capellen* in Ermanglung der Personen wol ausgelassen werden/ weil sie von dem *Concert*isten ohne dem schon mitgesungen werden." Fuhrmann, *Musicalischer-Trichter*, 80.

59. Walther, *Musicalisches Lexicon*, 130; quoted and translated in Snyder, *Dieterich Buxtehude*, 364.

60. "Ich hatte mir zwar vorgesetzet/ unterschiedene *Capellen* an dem meisten Theile dieser meiner *Evangelien* auszuzuziehen: Indem aber das Werck über Verhoffen mir unter den Händen gewachsen/ und groß worden/ wolte der jenige/ dem diese meine Arbeit gefiehle/ Ihme nicht zu entgegen seyn lassen/ selbe/ wo es vollstimmig/ herauß zu ziehen; Und so mans haben kan/ mit *Instrumenten* und duppelten *Vocalisten* zu bestellen." Andreas Hammerschmidt, *Ander Theil Geistlicher Gespräche über die Evangelia*. This quotation appears on a page under the heading "Günstiger Music-Liebhaber" in the *Sechste Stimme* partbook.

61. Barbara Wiermann has suggested that Hammerschmidt may have had two partbooks printed to simplify the addition of extra voices. Barbara Wiermann, *Die Entwicklung vokal-instrumentalen Komponierens im protestantischen Deutschland bis zur Mitte des 17. Jahrhunderts*, Abhandlungen der Musikgeschichte 14 (Göttingen: Vandenhoeck & Ruprecht, 2005), 61–62.

62. *MGG2*, Personenteil, s.v. "Büttner, Michael" (cols. 1435–36), by Greta Konradt; and Wiermann, *Entwicklung des vokal-instrumentalen Komponierens*, 356–62.

63. For examples of compositions with these types of emendations, see ibid., 476–83. Wiermann's research shows that strings and the *Posaunenchor* were the instruments most frequently added, though cornetts and trombones were the most popular additions to Hammerschmidt's works. See ibid., 362.

64. Ibid., 356–58. Although Wiermann's book does not refer to Ms. mus. 150, it includes an example of the music script of both Büttner and his copyist assistant on page 357, which matches the Bohn parts in this edition. Barbara Wiermann, e-mail message to author, 13 June 2008.

65. *NG2*, s.v. "Zeutschner, Tobias" (p. 797), by Werner Braun. Composer, organist, and poet, Zeutschner (1621–75) worked in Breslau as a schoolmaster and organist at St. Bernhardin from 1649, after which he became second organist at St. Maria Magdalena in 1655. Reinhold Starke, "Kantoren und Organisten der Kirche zu St. Maria Magdalena zu Breslau," in *Monatshefte für Musik-Geschichte*, ed. Robert Eitner, vol. 37, no. 6/7 (Leipzig: Breitkopf & Härtel, 1904), 100. Zeutschner's music is represented by Ms. mus. 210–351 in the Bohn collection.

66. Organist at St. Bernhardin from 1675, Mayer composed a complete liturgical cycle of concerted church music for large ensembles of voices and instruments, with titles including suggestions for varying the number of parts. Two of these pieces are named as dialogues ("Dialogus de Joseph" for Good Friday and "Zu der Zeit Herodes, des Königs" for the feast of John the Baptist), and two others identify characters ("Da Jesus gebohren war zu Bethlehem" for New Year and "Es begab sich aber, dass ein Geboth" for Christmas). For the list of all eighty-three compositions with liturgical day and instrumentation, see Emil Bohn, *Die musikalischen Handschriften des XVI. und XVII. Jahrhunderts in der Stadtbibliothek zu Breslau* (Breslau: Julius Heinauer, 1890), 157–63. Mayer's music is found in Ms. mus. 171 of the Bohn collection.

67. All five of Büttner's pieces call for large ensembles, with multiple choirs of soloists and capellen. Bohn miscounted the number of parts for *Der Herr* as twenty-seven. Büttner's music is catalogued as Ms. mus. 132; see ibid., 136. See also Wiermann, *Entwicklung des vokal-instrumentalen Komponierens*, 371. The capella parts were copied by the same hand as for Ms. mus. 150 and sport the same titles for the trombone parts: "Altus Voce è Trombin," "1 Tenor Voce è Trombon," and "Bassus Voce è Trombono."

68. Ms. mus. 150a also contains music by Hammerschmidt described as "Part. in Tab." from the printed collection *Fest- Buss- und Dancklieder* (Dresden, 1659). See Bohn, *Die musikalischen Handschriften*, 139–42.

69. *Musicalischer Andachten, Ander Theill* (Freiberg: Georg Beuther, 1641; repr., 1650 and 1659).

70. According to Praetorius, the bombardo is a regular bass shawm. Praetorius, *Syntagma musicum II: De Organographia Parts I and II*, 47. Fuhrmann defines it as a sixteen-foot instrument excellent for reinforcing a fundamental bass. Fuhrmann, *Musicalischer-Trichter*, 91–92.

71. Eleven pieces include one or two parts that double portions of more than one of the original prints, both instrumental and vocal.

72. Thirty compositions include a total of forty-one newly composed parts, the vast majority of which are for tenor voice and trombone and usually fulfill the function of a second tenor line added to a texture that already has one tenor part. These statistics do not include the six parts composed for the sinfonia added to the beginning of "Herr kom hinab."

73. Although the cornett is not a brass instrument, it will be referred to as such because it was a traditional *Stadtpfeiffer* instrument normally grouped with trombones and has a cup-shaped mouthpiece.

74. Wiermann has provided a ground plan of the church with the placement of choirs for the performance of music for Jubilate Sunday as prescribed by Breslau businessman Friedrich Cremitz, who left a legacy to support this performance annually from 1669 on. The first group consisted of the cantor, ten singers, organ, and violone; the second, six violins, four violas, and one bassoon; the third, four trombones, two cornetts, and organ; the fourth, two groups of two clarini, one *Principal*, one *Ducade* (all types of trumpets), and two timpani; and the fifth, four viole da gamba, one small bass violin, four recorders, and one crumhorn. Wiermann, *Entwicklung des vokal-instrumentalen Komponierens*, 352–55.

75. "Viel sind beruffen" and "O Jesu wir wissen, daß du" also have extra tablature, but there are not enough instrumental parts to create a third choir.

76. Two cornetts and four trombones are found in the pay records for the 1668 performance of Mayer's music for Jubilate Sunday, which also list the instrumentation by choirs. Max Schneider, "Die Besetzung der vielstimmigen Musik des 17. und 16. Jahrhunderts," *Archiv für Musikwissenschaft* 1 (1918/19): 223.

77. Martin Luther, *Lectures on the Minor Prophets III: Zechariah*, ed. Hilton C. Oswald, vol. 20, *Luther's Works*, ed. Jaroslav Pelikan (St. Louis: Concordia, 1973; electronic ed., *Luther's Works on CD-ROM*).

78. Luke 2:48–49 was set by a number of Hammerschmidt's contemporaries. In Schütz's setting of this story (SWV 401 from *Symphonarium sacrarum III*, 1650) Mary is a cantus, Joseph a bassus, and Jesus a cantus, and they are accompanied by two violins, continuo, and a four-part *complementum* of voices and instruments. The alternation between the parents, the use of descending thirds on "Mein Sohn," and the echoing of Jesus's words by the violins may have inspired Hammerschmidt's composition. However, Schütz concluded the work with Psalm 84:1–2, 4 ("Wie lieblich sind deine Wohnungen"). Tilley describes and provides a score of Augustin Pfleger's "Siehe, dein Vater und ich" for CCB, three violas, violone, and continuo. Pfleger (ca. 1635–90) interpolated other Gospel texts as well as excerpts from the Song of Solomon into his version, and the strings tend to accompany Joseph, a bassus. Tilley, "Dialogue Techniques," 206–15 and 298–313. She lists a further setting by Stephan Otto (1603–56) entitled "Mein Sohn/ warumb hast du uns das gethan" for CAB and continuo. Ibid., 240.

79. There are three pieces from the 1656 collection that call for five strings and clavicembalo. In each case the clavicembalo serves as continuo for the string choir, which is used in tuttis and in imitation or alternation with a voice representing the mature Christ, not the boy.

80. Diana Rothaug has suggested that the two cantus represent two believers, who see a parallel between their life and that of the centurion. Diana Rothaug, " 'Unser aller Bild und Spiegel': Andreas Hammerschmidts *Musicalische Gespräche über die Evangelia* und die Schriftauslegung seiner Zeit," in *Ständige Konferenz Mitteldeutsche Barockmusik in Sachsen, Sachsen-Anhalt und Thüringen*, Jahrbuch 1999, ed. Wilhelm Seidel (Eisenach: Karl Dieter Wagner, 2000), 36.

81. Tilley and Märker both list a setting by Sebastian Knüpfer (1633–76), "Herr, hilf uns, wir verderben," for CATB, two violins, two violas, continuo, and possibly bassoon. See Tilley, "Dialogue Techniques," 249; and Märker, *Die protestantische Dialogkomposition*, 100. Tilley also describes and supplies a score of a setting by Briegel, "Herr hilff uns" for CCTTB, two violins, and continuo. Briegel's version interpolates poetry and incorporates a chorale melody and verse into the biblical story. Tilley, "Dialogue Techniques," 144–56 and 278–97.

82. "While he abandons us he is upholding us and while he is allowing us to go through storms in terror he is bringing us forward. Thus he brings it about that we do not perish but rather turn back to him, so that more and more we are constantly being saved. Indeed, he wants to arouse in us a desire for him, so that we may continue to cry out to him; he wants us to cry out to him in order that he may hear and answer us." Martin Luther, *Sermons I*, ed. John W. Doberstein, vol. 51, *Luther's Works*, ed. Helmut Lehmann (Philadelphia: Fortress Press, 1959; electronic ed., *Luther's Works on CD-ROM*).

83. Briegel also set this text for the same Sunday in his *Erster Theil Evangelischer Gespräch*, interpolating poetry between the biblical verses and at the end to dramatize the story. This piece also receives capella parts that are now in the Bohn collection, Ms. mus. 130. The work is scored for two violins, CCTTB, and continuo, with capella parts of CCTB that are used in tutti sections of the last third of the work, in the same manner as described above under the third use of capella parts. See Bohn, *Die musikalischen Handschriften*, 128–29.

84. Tilley has argued that the Lazarus story served to teach seventeenth-century Lutherans how to die, as well as how to live. Janette Tilley, "Learning from Lazarus: The Rich Man and Lazarus Parable and the Seventeenth-Century Lutheran Art of Dying," *Early Music History* 28 (2009): 184.

85. Johann Rudolf Ahle (*Erster Theil Geistlichen Dialogen*, 1648) and Schütz (SWV 477, ca. 1640–50) each set this text as well, though Ahle's setting offers only two verses (Luke 16:24–25). Both Ahle and Hammerschmidt used the bassus to represent Abraham, although Ahle's rich man is a tenor. Schütz's rich man is a bassus, while his Abraham is a tenor. Ahle's accompaniment consists only of continuo, whereas Schütz uses two violins to accompany the rich man, two transverse flutes to accompany Abraham, and a finale for two angels, Lazarus and Abraham (CCAT). Tilley has described two other settings of this story. One is the anonymous "Es war ein reicher Mann, Dialogo von reichen Manne" for CCTTBB, two violins, and two continuo, and the other is by Andreas Fromm (1621–83), called "Actus musicus de Divite et Lazaro" for fourteen voices in two choirs, nine instruments, and continuo found in *Denkmäler der Musik in Pommern*, vol. 5, ed. Hans Engel, (Kassel: Bärenreiter, 1936). See Tilley, "Dialogue Techniques," 72–77. Märker's study mentions a setting by Thomas Selle, "Es war aber ein reicher Mann" for ATB, 2 violins, and continuo. See Märker, *Die protestantische Dialogkomposition*, 32.

86. According to Wackernagel, this chorale was sung to the tune of Martin Luther's "Nun frewt euch lieben Christen gemein." Ringwald's setting is a revision of an older text. Philipp Wackernagel, *Das deutsche Kirchenlied von der ältesten Zeit bis zu Anfang des XVII. Jahrhunderts*, 5 vols. (Leipzig, 1864; repr., Hildesheim: Georg Olms Verlagsbuchhandlung, 1964), 4:344–45. The text to the first verse of "Es ist gewisslich an der Zeit" is derived from the sequence *Dies irae*, thus confirming the connection to the day of judgement.

87. The instrumentation of both pieces provides a significant timbral change towards the end of each half of the church year. Both works share a harmonic focus around E minor/major and a melancholy *Affekt*.

88. Winterfeld has speculated that Hammerschmidt wrote the melodies. Winterfeld, *Der Evangelische Kirchengesang*, 2:264.

89. As with "O Vater, aller Augen warten auff dich" and "Gott fähret auff mit Jauchtzen!" the trombono grosso serves as a third trombone whenever the two trombones of the print are present, forming a trio.

90. Leonard, introduction to *Seventeenth-Century Lutheran Church Music*, xiii; Tilley, introduction to Andreas Hammerschmidt, *Geistlicher Dialogen Ander Theil*, xiii; Michael Praetorius, *Syntagma musicum*, vol. 2, *De Organographia*, parts 4–5 (period organs and stops), 119–60; and vol. 3, *Termini musici*, part 3, chapter 6 (figures and realization), 161–203 (Wolfenbüttel, 1619; facsimile repr., ed. Arno Forchert, Kassel: Bärenreiter, 2001). See also Franck Thomas Arnold, *The Art of Accompaniment from a Thorough-Bass: As Practiced in the XVII and XVIII Centuries*, 2 vols. (1931; repr., New York: Dover, 1965), 1:1–239.

91. The term "traversa" was used to indicate that a transverse flute was required. For example, Tobias Michael called for both "flauto" and "traversa" in his "Wo der Herr nicht" from *Musicalischer Seelen-Lust Ander Theil* (1637). See Charlotte A. Leonard, "The Role of the Trombone and its *Affekt* in the Lutheran Church Music of Seventeenth-Century Saxony and

Thuringia: The Early Seventeenth Century," *Historic Brass Society Journal* 10 (1998): 61. In this instance, the recorder played the higher part.

92. Praetorius, *Syntagma musicum II: De Organographia Parts I and II*, 35 and 43. The highest pitch required by a trombone in these pieces is normally a', and the lowest pitch required is D. However, "O Vater, aller Augen warten auff dich" requires b♭', which modern tenor trombone players are expected to be able to play.

93. Ibid., 43. This is confirmed by Johann Rudolf Ahle's description "*Trombone Majore, Grosso, Grando, Quart* oder *Quint Posaun*." See Ahle, index to *Brevis et perspicua introductio in artem musicam*. Johann Georg Ahle retained his father's description. Ahle, *Kurze doch deutliche Anleitung zu der lieblichen und löblichen Singekunst*, 32.

94. "Können die *Concert*-Stimmen und *favoritten*, in etwas von den *Capellen* abgesondert werden: Doch nicht so gar weit/ wie etliche im gebrauch haben/ welches eines iedwedern Bescheidenheit anheim gestellet wird. So wird auch ein ieder die Gelegenheit des Orts in acht zu nehmen wissen/ und sonderlich darauff trachten/ daß nicht eine stumme Andacht verursachet/ sondern vor allen Dingen der Text klar und deutlich außgesprochen und vernommen werde: Inmassen denn an etzlichen vornehmen Orten man nach Gelegenheit des Gesanges/ solchen/ umb die Wort besser zu vernehmen/ mitten in der Kirchen bey einem Regal anzustellen pfleget." Andreas Hammerschmidt, "An den Music Liebhabenden Leser," in *Vierdter Theil, Musicalischer Andachten, Geistlicher Moteten und Concerten* (Freiberg: Georg Beuther, 1646). Translation based on Schmidt, "Musicalische Andachten," 175. and revised with assistance from Howard Weiner.

95. Hammerschmidt, "An den Music Liebhabenden Leser," in *Vierdter Theil, Musicalischer Andachten, Geistlicher Moteten und Concerten*; quoted and translated in ibid. Hammerschmidt cited "Herr höre, und sey mir gnädig" as an exception to this policy. The work is available in Leonard, *Seventeenth-Century Lutheran Church Music*, 65–79.

96. "Ich . . . [werde] dieselbe nach Gelegenheit zu *dirigiren* und im besten entweder *Vocaliter* oder *Instrumentaliter* anzustellen/ eines jedweden *discretion* anheim geben." Andreas Hammerschmidt, "Günstiger lieber Leser," *Musicalischer Andachten, Ander Theill, Das ist Geistliche Madrigalien Mit 4. 5. und 6. Stimmen sambt einem General-Baß Benebenst einer Fünffstimmigen Capella so nach beliebung gebrauch oder außen gelassen werden kan* (Freyberg in Meissen: Georg Beuther, 1641). The fact that a five-part capella may be included or excluded in the performance of the pieces in this collection is made clear in the full title, which notes that the capella "can be used or left out at will."

97. Hammerschmidt, *Musicalischer Andacht, Erster Theil* (Freiberg: Georg Beuther, 1638); quoted and translated in Schmidt, "Musicalische Andachten," 78; modified with assistance from Bettina Brockerhoff-Macdonald.

98. Hammerschmidt, preface to *Vierdter Theil, Musicalischer Andachten, Geistlicher Moteten und Concerten*; quoted and translated in Snyder, *Dieterich Buxtehude*, 150.

99. Hammerschmidt, preface to *Vierdter Theil Musicalische Andachten*; quoted and translated in Schmidt, "Musicalische Andachten," 175.

100. Mueller, "Musicalische Gespräche," 139.

101. Tilley, introduction to Andreas Hammerschmidt, *Geistlicher Dialogen*, xiii.

102. Quoted and translated in Mueller, "Musicalische Gespräche," 139–40.

103. Cleveland Johnson, *Vocal Compositions in German Organ Tablatures, 1550–1650: A Catalogue and Commentary* (New York: Garland, 1989), 62 and 64.

104. The *Tabulaturbuch* (1583) of Rühling (1550–1615) organizes sacred compositions by various composers into a liturgical cycle. The *Thesaurus Motetarum* (1589) of Paix (fl. 1585) presents in chronological order the sacred works of various composers, including one of Paix's own pieces. The *Nova Musices Organicae Tabulatura* (1617) of Johann Woltz (c. 1550–1618) combines fugues and *canzoni* with a liturgical cycle. Ibid., 102 and 108–10.

105. Ibid., 61 and 126.

106. For a thorough explanation of the purpose and use of intabulations by German organists in the early baroque period see ibid., 123–47.

107. "Wie ich dann unterschiedliche *Directores* gekennet, die ihre *Partituren* in teutsche *Tabulatur* gesetzet, und daraus gesungen, und *dirigiret*. Ich kann auch noch mit des vornehmen *Grimmii* eigener Hand bezeugen, daß Er aus der deutschen *Tabulatur*, oder Buchstaben *dirigiret* hat." Andreas Werckmeister, *Musicalische Paradoxal Discourse* (1707), 72; quoted in Johnson, *Vocal Compositions in German Organ Tablatures*, 126. Grimmii refers to Heinrich Grimm (1592/3– 1637), a student of Michael Praetorius and a composer of Lutheran church music.

108. Johnson, *Vocal Compositions in German Organ Tablatures*, 131 and 133.

109. Bohn, *Die musikalischen Handschriften*, 139.

110. Although he names no specific pieces, Johnson states that figured bass lines for some compositions by Hammerschmidt are found in the Staatsbibliothek zu Berlin – Preußischer Kulturbesitz, Mus. ms. 40075. See Johnson, *Vocal Compositions in German Organ Tablatures*, 70. Fragmentary or incomplete intabulations of five works from *Musicalischer Andachten, Ander Theill* (1641) are in Warsaw, Biblioteka Narodowa, Mus. 326. See ibid., 95. Johnson's study also provides catalogues of Mus. ms. 40075 and Mus. 326 in a separately-paginated appendix; see pages 30 and 260.

111. Both Jacob Handl's "Alleluia" and Hieronymus Praetorius's "Herr Gott, dich loben wir" were performed with the organ alone named as one of the choirs at a chapel dedication service. Frederick Kent Gable, introduction to *Dedication Service for St. Gertrude's Chapel, Hamburg, 1607*, Recent Researches in the Music of the Baroque Era, vol. 91 (Madison: A-R Editions, 1998), viii and xviii. Michael Praetorius also referred to this practice in the polychoral performance of chorales, noting that an organ, positive, or regal could replace instruments if necessary. Michael Praetorius, *Urania (1613)*, ed. Friedrich Blume, Gesamtausgabe der Musikalischen Werke von Michael Praetorius, vol. 16 (Wolfenbüttel: Möseler Verlag, 1928–41), x.

Texts and Translations

Biblical translations and punctuation have been made with the assistance of *Die Bibel oder die ganze Heilige Schrift des Alten und Neuen Testaments nach der deutschen Übersetzung Martin Luthers Textfassung 1912* (hereafter cited as *DB*) and the *New Revised Standard Version Bible* (hereafter cited as *NRSV*). Hammerschmidt followed closely the text of Martin Luther's translation of the Bible, with some omissions and additions. Significant departures from the Bible appear in the comments. Chorale texts and punctuation were prepared with the assistance of Philipp Wackernagel, *Das deutsche Kirchenlied von der ältesten Zeit bis zu Anfang des XVII. Jahrhunderts* (hereafter cited as Wackernagel), 5 vols. (Leipzig, 1864; repr., Hildesheim: Georg Olms Verlagsbuchhandlung, 1964).

Freue dich, du Tochter Zion

Freue dich, du Tochter Zion, und du, Tochter Jerusalem, jauchze!

Siehe, dein König kommt zu dir sanfftmütig und reitet auff einem Esel.

Hosianna dem Sohne David! Gelobet sey, der da kommt in Namen des Herren! Hosianna in der Höhe!
(Zech. 9:9; Matt. 21:5, 9)

Rejoice, Daughter of Zion

Rejoice greatly, O daughter Zion! And shout aloud, O daughter Jerusalem!

Look, your king comes to you, humble, and riding on a donkey.

Hosanna to the Son of David! Praise be to he who comes in the name of the Lord! Hosanna in the highest!

Mein Sohn, warumb hast du uns das gethan?

Mein Sohn, warumb hast du uns das gethan? Je mein Sohn, warumb hast du uns das gethan? Siehe, dein Vater und ich haben dich mit Schmertzen gesucht. Deine Mutter, dein Vater haben dich mit Schmertzen gesucht.

Was ists, daß ihr mich gesucht habt? Wisset ihr nicht, daß ich seyn muß in dem, das meines Vaters ist?

Alleluja!
(Luke 2:48–49)

My son, why have you done this to us?

My son, why have you done this to us? O my son, why have you done this to us? Look, your father and I have been searching for you in great anxiety. Your mother, your father have been searching for you in great anxiety.

Why were you searching for me? Did you not know that I must be in my Father's house?

Alleluja!

Comment. "Deine Mutter" is an addition that draws attention to the three-person conversation between Jesus (altus) and his parents (cantus and bassus).

Herr, ich bin nicht werth

Herr, ich bin nicht werth, daß du unter mein Dach eingehest; sprich nur ein Wort, so wird meine Seele gesund.

Ich bin der Herr, dein Artzt.
Sey getrost; deine Sünde sind dir vergeben.
Gehe hin; dir geschehe, wie du gegläubet hast.

Lord, I am not worthy

Lord, I am not worthy to have you come under my roof; but only speak the word, and my soul will be healed.

I am the Lord, your healer.
Have faith; your sins will be forgiven.
Go; let it be done for you, according to your faith.

Meine Seele, lobe den Herren, und vergiß nicht, was er dir Guts gethan hat: der dir alle deine Sünde vergiebet und heilet alle deine Gebrechen.
(Matt. 8:8; Exod. 15:26; Matt. 9:2; Matt. 8:13; Ps. 103:2–3)

My soul, praise the Lord, and do not forget what good he has done for you, who forgives all your sins and heals all your afflictions.

Comment. Matthew 8:8 has "Knecht gesund" rather than "Seele gesund."

O Herr hilf, wir verderben!

O Herr hilf, wir verderben!
Meister, Meister, wir verderben!
Meister, fragst du nichts darnach, wir verderben!

O ihr Kleingläubigen, wo ist euer Glaube?
Wind und Meer schweig und verstumme!

Was ist das für ein Mann, dem Wind und Meer gehorsam ist?

Alleluja!
(Matt. 8:25–27)

O Lord save us, we are perishing!

O Lord save us, we are perishing!
Master, Master, we are perishing!
Master, do you not question this, we are perishing!

O you of little faith, where is your faith?
Wind and sea be silent and cease!

What sort of man is this, that the wind and the sea obey him?

Alleluja!

Comments. Matthew 8:26 has "Warum seid ihr so furchtsam" instead of "Wo ist euer Glaube." Perhaps in order to avoid the shift in speaker and provide more text for Jesus (bassus) to sing, the command "Wind und Meer schweig und verstumme" replaces "Und stand auf und bedrohte den Wind und das Meer; da ward es ganz stille" (Matt. 8:26). The Hammerschmidt print and Bohn capella parts have "Was ist das vor ein Mann," whereas most German bibles from Hammerschmidt's time have "Was ist das für ein Mann," reflecting a seventeenth-century tendency to use "vor" and "für" interchangeably. The modern "für" has been selected for this edition.

O Vater, aller Augen warten auff dich

O Vater, aller Augen warten auff dich.

Werdet ihr meine Gebothe halten, so wil ich euch Regen geben zu seiner Zeit, das Land soll sein Gewächse geben, die Bäume auff dem Felde sollen ihre Früchte bringen, ihr sollet Brods die Fülle haben.

O Vater, du thust deine milde Hand auff, du sättigest alles, was da lebet.

Dancket dem Herren; denn er ist freundlich, seine Güte währet ewiglich.
(Ps. 145:15; Lev. 26:3–4, 5b; Ps. 145:16; Ps. 106:1)

O Father, the eyes of all look to you

O Father, the eyes of all look to you.

If you keep my commandments, I will give you your rains in their season, the land shall yield its produce, the trees of the field shall yield their fruit, you shall eat your bread to the full.

O Father, you open your benevolent hand, you satisfy the desire of every living thing.

O give thanks to the Lord, for he is kind; his goodness endures forever.

Comment. Psalm 145:16 has "erfüllest alles, was lebt, mit Wohlgefallen," rather than "du sättigest alles, was da lebet."

Gott fähret auff mit Jauchtzen!

Gott fähret auff mit Jauchtzen! Frolocket mit Händen, alle Völcker. Frolocket mit Händen und jauchtzet Gott mit frölichen Schalle!
Denn der Herr, der Allerhöchste, ist erschrecklich, ein grosser König auff den gantzen Erdboden.
Er wird die Völcker unter uns zwingen und die Leute unter unsre Füsse. Er erwehlet uns zum Erbtheil, die Herrligkeit Jacob, den er liebet. Sela.

God has gone up with a shout!

God has gone up with a shout! Clap your hands, all you peoples. Clap your hands and shout to God with joyous sounds!
For the Lord, the Most High is awesome, a great king over all the earth.
He will subdue peoples under us and nations under our feet. He chose our heritage for us, the pride of Jacob, whom he loves. *Selah.*

Gott fähret auff mit Jauchtzen und der Herr mit heller Posaunen. Lobsinget Gott, lobsinget unserm Könige! Alleluja!	God has gone up with a shout and the Lord with bright trombone. Sing praises to God, sing praises to our King! Allelujah!
(Ps. 47:2–7)	(Ps. 47:1–6)

Comments. NRSV has "trumpet" for "Posaunen." The Hebrew psalm text specifies "shofar" (ram's horn), which is traditionally rendered as "Posaune" in German and "trumpet" in English.

Vater Abraham / *Father Abraham*

Vater Abraham, erbarme dich mein und sende Lazarum, daß er das Eußerste seines Fingers ins Wasser tauche und kühle meine Zunge; denn ich leide Pein in dieser Flammen.	Father Abraham, have mercy on me and send Lazarus, that he dip the tip of his finger in water and cool my tongue; for I am in agony in these flames.
Gedencke, Sohn, daß du dein Guts empfangen hast in deinem Leben, und Lazarus dagegen hat Böses empfangen; nun aber wird er getröstet, und du wirst gepeiniget.	Remember, son, that you received your good things during your lifetime, and Lazarus in like manner received evil things; but now he is comforted, and you are in agony.
Und über das alles ist zwischen uns und euch eine grosse Klufft befestiget, daß die da wolten von hinnen hinabfahren zu euch, können nicht, und auch nicht von dannen zu uns herüberfahren.	And besides all this between us and you a great chasm has been fixed, so that those who might want to pass from here to you cannot do so, and no one can cross from there to us.
So bitt ich dich, Vater, sende Lazarum in meines Vaters Hauß; denn ich habe noch fünff Brüder, daß er ihnen bezeuge, auff daß sie nicht auch kommen an diesen Orth der Qual.	Then I beg you father, send Lazarus to my father's house; for I have five brothers, that he may warn them, so that they will not also come into this place of torment.
Sie haben Mosen und die Propheten; laß sie dieselbigen hören.	They have Moses and the prophets; they should listen to them.
Nein, nein, Vater Abraham! Sondern wenn einer von den Toden zu ihnen ging, so würden sie Busse thun.	No, no, father Abraham! But if someone goes to them from the dead, they would do penance.
Hören sie Mosen und die Propheten nicht, so werden sie auch nicht gläuben, ob jemand von den Toden aufferstünde.	If they do not listen to Moses and the prophets, neither will they be convinced, even if someone rises from the dead.
(Luke 16:24–31)	

Comment. This setting omits the words of the biblical narrator.

Es wird eine grosse Trübsal seyn / *There will be great tribulation*

Es wird eine grosse Trübsal seyn, als nicht gewesen ist von Anfang der Welt biß her und als auch nicht werden wird.	There will be great tribulation, such has not been, from the beginning of the world until now, and also never will be.
Und wo die Tage nicht würden verkürtzet, so würde kein Mensch selig; umb der Außerwehlten willen werden die Tage verkürtzet.	And if the days had not been cut short, no one would be saved; but for the sake of the elect, those days will be cut short.
(Matt. 24:21–22)	
O Jesu Christ, du machst es lang mit deinem Jüngsten Tage! Den Leuten wird auff Erden bang von wegen vieler Plage. Kom doch, kom doch, du Richter groß, und mach uns in der Gnaden loß von allem Übel! Amen.	O Jesus Christ, you delay your days of judgement! The people on earth become anxious because of much vexation, Surely you will still come, great judge, and by your grace free us from all evil! Amen.
(Bartholomäus Ringwald)	

Comment. The chorale verse, which commences with the text "O Jesu Christ," is verse 7 of the chorale "Es ist gewisslich an der Zeit" by Bartholomäus Ringwald, published in *Geistliche Lieder und Gebetlein* (Frankfurt an der Oder, 1586; see Wackernagel 4:345, no. 491). It is interpolated into the text from Matthew 24.

Plates

Plate 1. Andreas Hammerschmidt, *Musicalische Gespräche über die Evangelia* (Dresden, 1655), partbook 6, title page. Dresden, Sächsische Landesbibliothek – Staats- und Universitätsbibliothek, Mus Gri 39, 1. Reproduced with permission from the Sächsische Landesbibliothek – Staats- und Universitätsbibliothek.

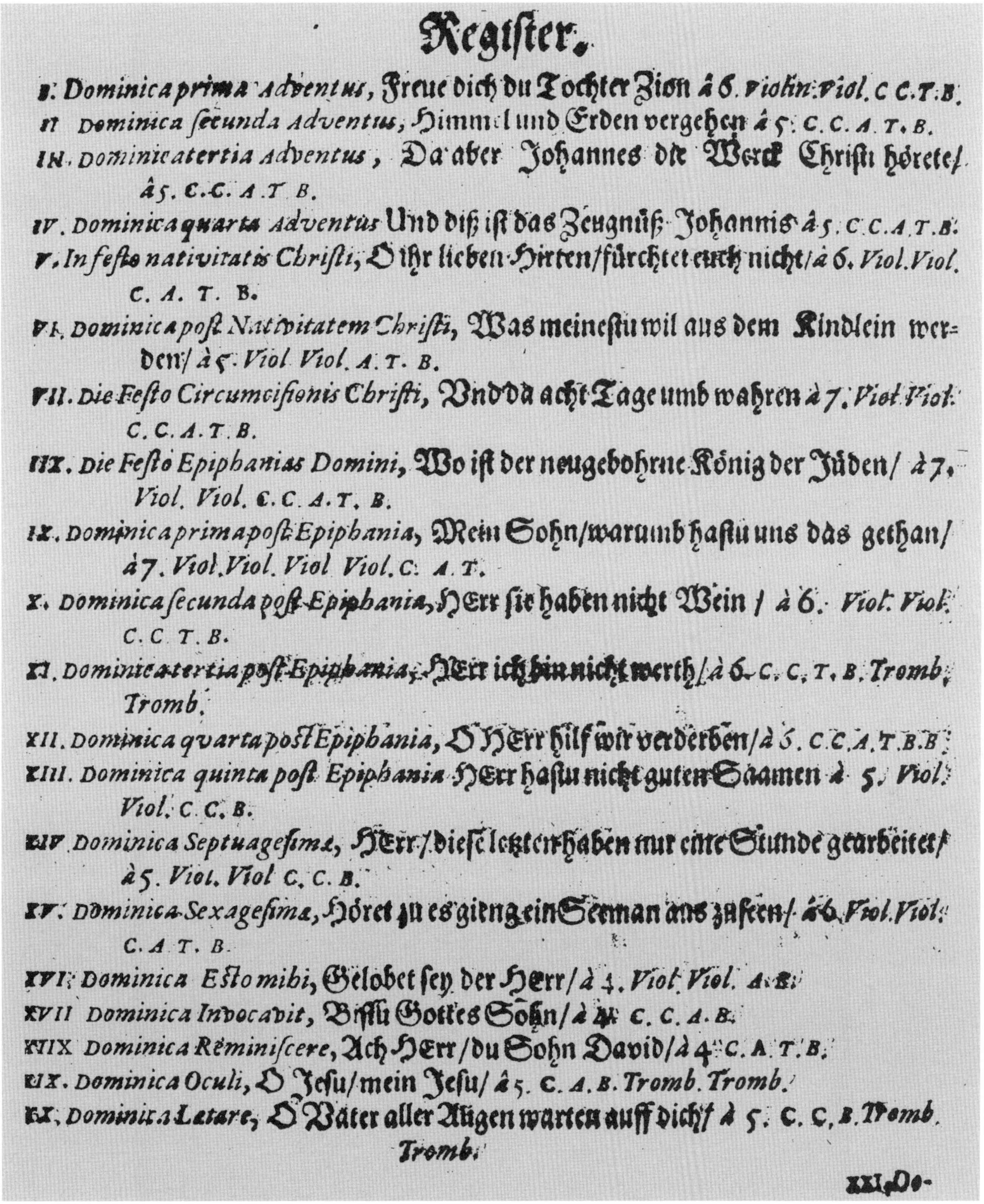

Register.

I. Dominica prima Adventus, Freue dich du Tochter Zion à 6. Violin. Viol. C C. T. B.

II. Dominica secunda Adventus, Himmel und Erden vergehen à 5. C.C. A. T. B.

III. Dominica tertia Adventus, Da aber Johannes die Werck Christi höretet/ à 5. C.C. A. T. B.

IV. Dominica quarta Adventus Und diß ist das Zeugnuß Johannis à 5. C.C. A. T. B.

V. In festo nativitatis Christi, O ihr lieben Hirten/fürchtet euch nicht/à 6. Viol. Viol. C. A. T. B.

VI. Dominica post Nativitatem Christi, Was meinestu wil aus dem Kindlein werden/ à 5. Viol. Viol. A. T. B.

VII. Die Festo Circumcisionis Christi, Und da acht Tage umb wahren à 7. Viol. Viol. C. C. A. T. B.

IIX. Die Festo Epiphanias Domini, Wo ist der neugebohrne König der Jüden/ à 7. Viol. Viol. C. C. A. T. B.

IX. Dominica prima post Epiphania, Mein Sohn/warumb hastu uns das gethan/ à 7. Viol. Viol. Viol. Viol. C. A. T.

X. Dominica secunda post Epiphania, Herr sie haben nicht Wein / à 6. Viol. Viol. C. C. T. B.

XI. Dominica tertia post Epiphania, Herr ich bin nicht werth/à 6. C. C. T. B. Tromb. Tromb.

XII. Dominica qvarta post Epiphania, O Herr hilf wir verderben/à 6. C.C. A. T. B. B.

XIII. Dominica quinta post Epiphania Herr hastu nicht guten Saamen à 5. Viol. Viol. C. C. B.

XIV. Dominica Septuagesimæ, Herr/diese letzten haben nur eine Stunde gearbeitet/ à 5. Viol. Viol. C. C. B.

XV. Dominica Sexagesimæ, Höret zu es ging ein Seeman aus zu seen/ à 6. Viol. Viol. C. A. T. B.

XVI. Dominica Esto mihi, Gelobet sey der Herr/à 4. Viol. Viol. A. B.

XVII Dominica Invocavit, Bistu Gottes Sohn/à 4. C. C. A. B.

XIIX Dominica Reminiscere, Ach Herr/du Sohn David/à 4. C. A. T. B.

XIX. Dominica Oculi, O Jesu/mein Jesu/à 5. C. A. B. Tromb. Tromb.

XX. Dominica Lætare, O Väter aller Augen warten auff dich/ à 5. C. C. B. Tromb. Tromb.

XXI. Do-

Plate 2. Andreas Hammerschmidt, *Musicalische Gespräche über die Evangelia* (Dresden, 1655), partbook 6, first page of register. Dresden, Sächsische Landesbibliothek – Staats- und Universitätsbibliothek, Mus Gri 39, 1. Reproduced with permission from the Sächsische Landesbibliothek – Staats- und Universitätsbibliothek.

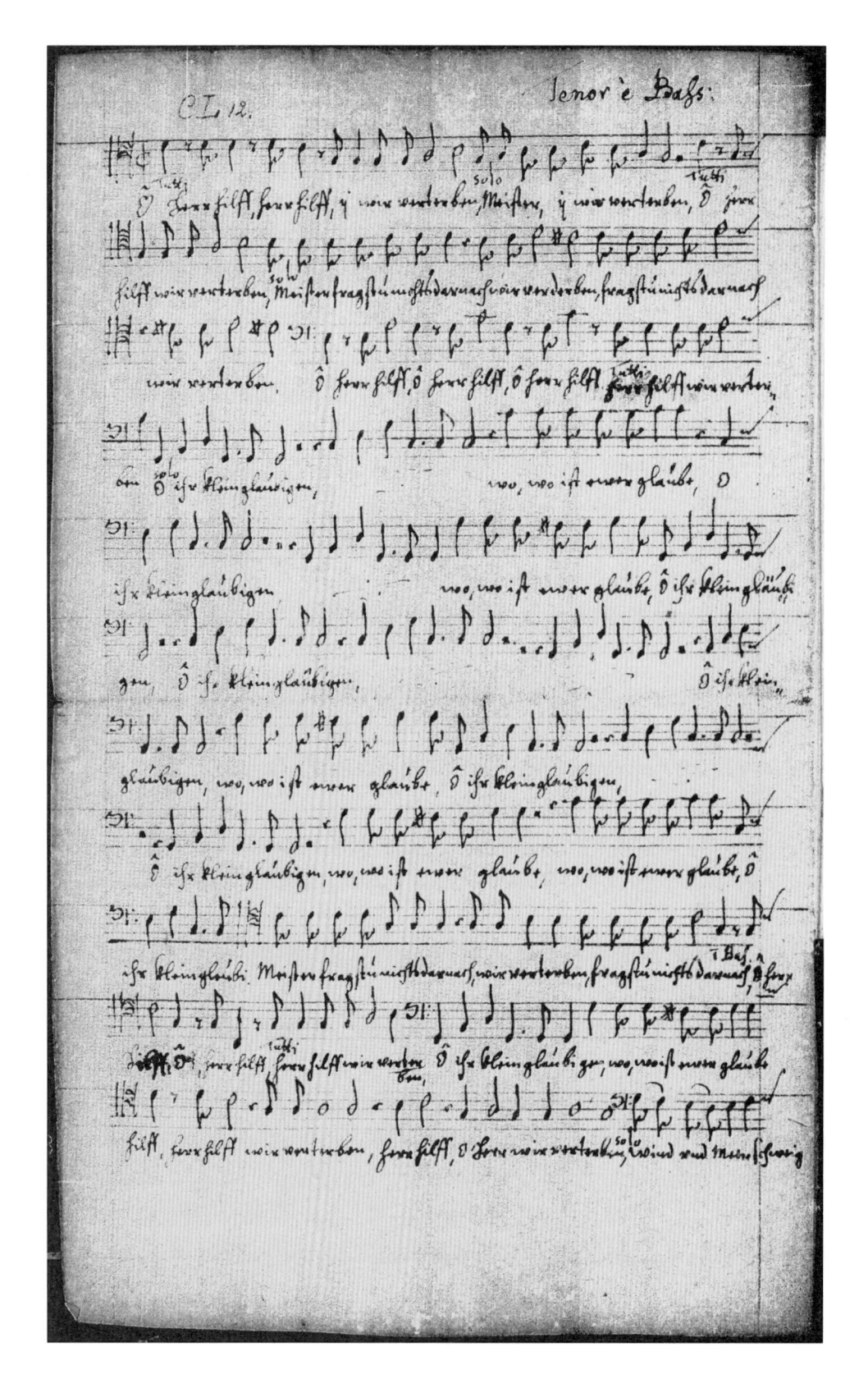

Plate 3. "O Herr hilf, wir verderben!" Tenor è Bass composite capella part. Berlin, Staatsbibliothek zu Berlin – Preußischer Kulturbesitz, Bohn Collection, Ms. mus. 150, no. 12, folio 44v. Reproduced with permission from the Staatsbibliothek zu Berlin – Preußischer Kulturbesitz.

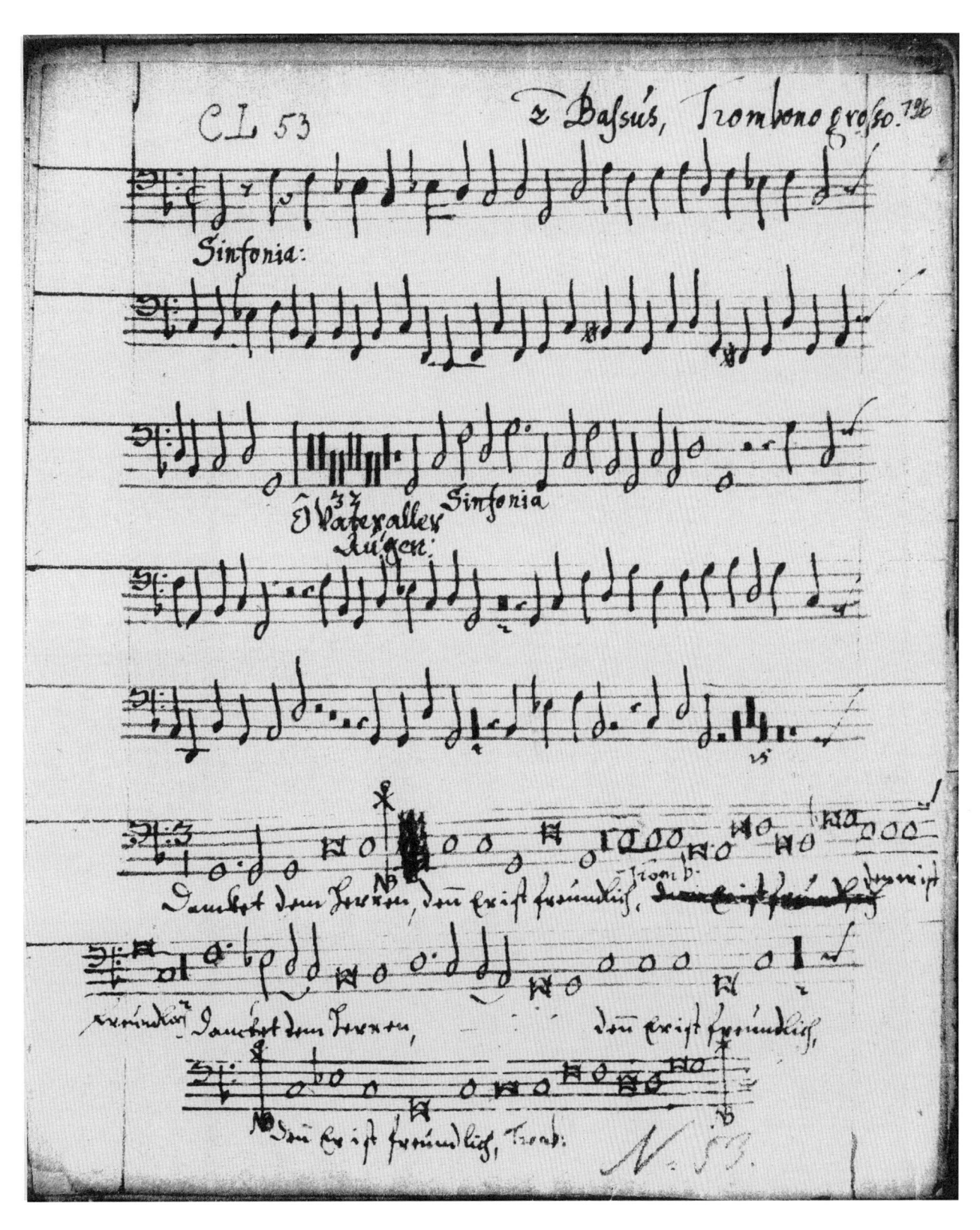

Plate 4. "O Vater, aller Augen warten auff dich," 2 Bassús, Trombono grosso capella part. Berlin, Staatsbibliothek zu Berlin – Preußischer Kulturbesitz, Bohn Collection, Ms. mus. 150, no. 53, folio 196r. Reproduced with permission from the Staatsbibliothek zu Berlin – Preußischer Kulturbesitz.

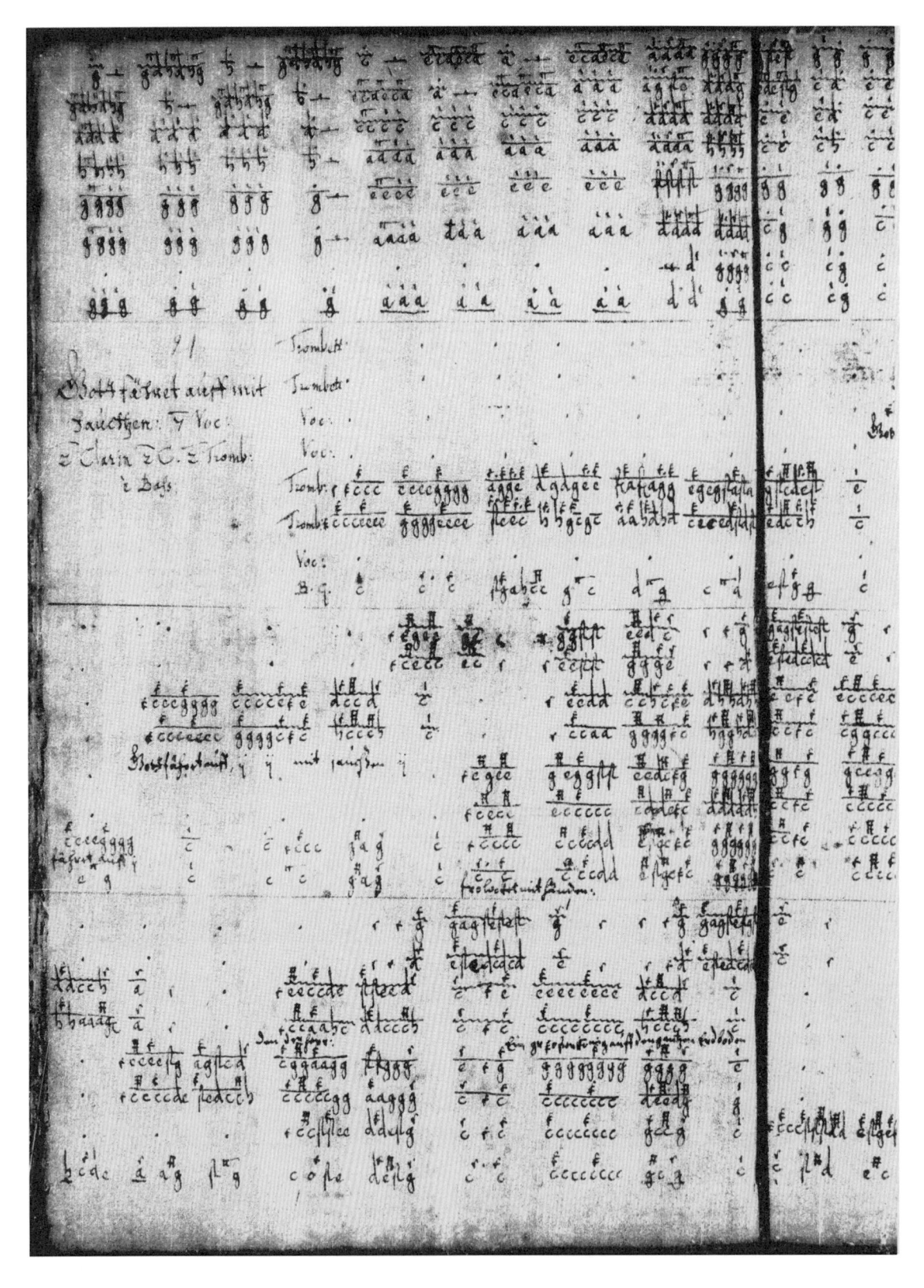

Plate 5. "Gott fähret auff mit Jauchtzen!" First page of organ tablature. Berlin, Staatsbibliothek zu Berlin – Preußischer Kulturbesitz, Bohn Collection, Ms. mus. 150, no. 21, folio 36v. Reproduced with permission from the Staatsbibliothek zu Berlin – Preußischer Kulturbesitz.

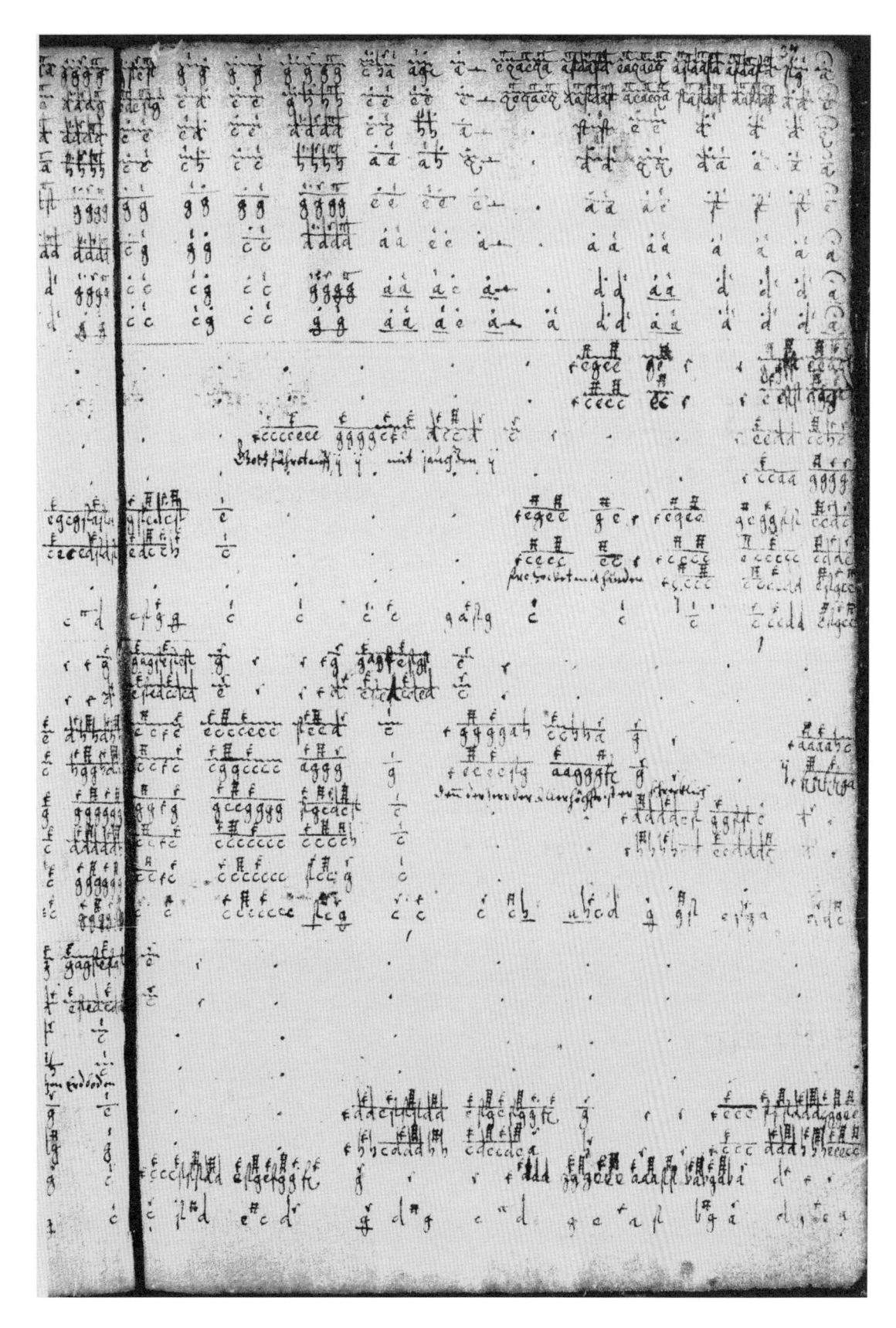

Plate 6. "Gott fähret auff mit Jauchtzen!" Second page of organ tablature. Berlin, Staatsbibliothek zu Berlin – Preußischer Kulturbesitz, Bohn Collection, Ms. mus. 150, no. 21, folio 37r. Reproduced with permission from the Staatsbibliothek zu Berlin – Preußischer Kulturbesitz.

Selections from the
Musicalische Gespräche über die Evangelia (1655) and
Ander Theil Geistlicher Gespräche über die Evangelia (1656)

Freue dich, du Tochter Zion

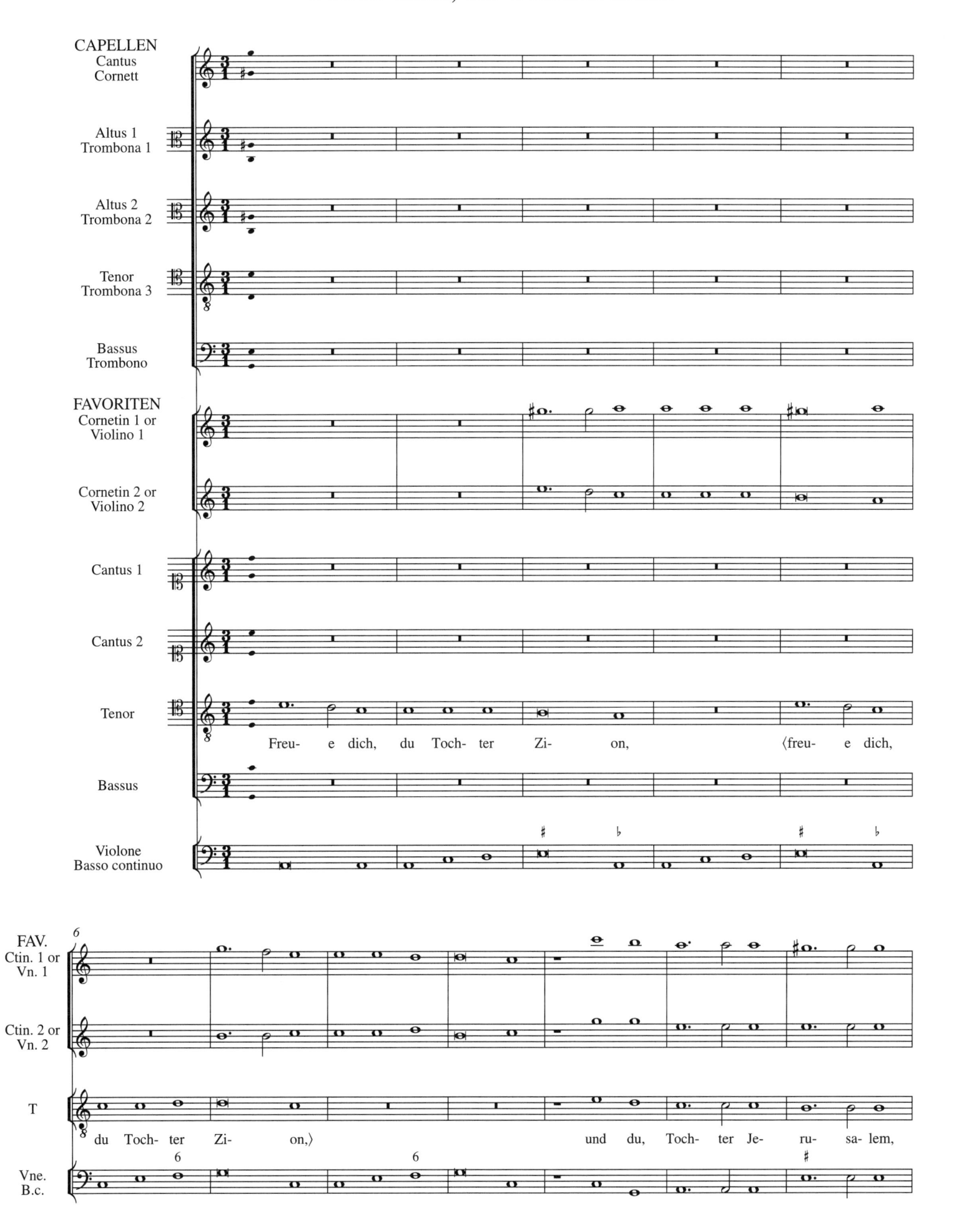

13
FAV.
Ctin. 1 or Vn. 1
Ctin. 2 or Vn. 2
T
jauch- - ze, jauch- ze, jauch- ze! Sie- he, dein Kö- nig kommt zu
Vne. B.c.
18
FAV.
T
dir sanfft- mü- tig, dein Kö- nig kommt zu dir, ⟨dein Kö- nig kommt zu dir⟩ sanfft- mü-
Vne. B.c.
22
CAP.
C Ct.
Ho- si-
A1 Trb. 1
Ho- si-
A2 Trb. 2
Ho- si-
T Trb. 3
Ho- si-
B Trbo.
Ho- si-
FAV.
Ctin. 1 or Vn. 1
Ctin. 2 or Vn. 2
C1
Ho- si- an- na, ⟨ho- si- an- na⟩ dem Soh- ne Da- vid! Ho- si-
C2
Ho- si- an- na, ⟨ho- si- an- na⟩ dem Soh- ne Da- vid! Ho- si-
T
-tig,
B
Ho- si- an- na, ⟨ho- si- an- na⟩ dem Soh- ne Da- vid! Ho- si- an- na, ⟨ho- si-
Vne. B.c.

26
CAP.
C
Ct.
-an- na, ho- si- an- na, ⟨ho- si- an- na,⟩ ho- si- an- na dem Soh- ne Da- vid!
A1
Trb. 1
-an- na, ho- si- an- na, ⟨ho- si- an- na, ho- si- an- na⟩ dem Soh- ne Da- vid!
A2
Trb. 2
-an- na, ho- si- an- na, ⟨ho- si- an- na, ho- si- an- na⟩ dem Soh- ne Da- vid!
T
Trb. 3
-an- na, ho- si- an- na, ⟨ho- si- an- na,⟩ ho- si- an- na⟩ dem Soh- ne Da- vid!
B
Trbo.
-an- na, ho- si- an- na, ⟨ho- si- an- na,⟩ ho- si- an- na dem Soh- ne Da- vid!
FAV.
Ctin. 1 or
Vn. 1
Ctin. 2 or
Vn. 2
C1
-an- na, ⟨ho- si- an- na, ho- si- an- na, ho- si- an- na⟩ dem Soh- ne Da- vid!
C2
-an- na, ⟨ho- si- an- na, ho- si- an- na, ho- si- an- na⟩ dem Soh- ne Da- vid!
T
B
-an- na, ho- si- an- na, ho- si- an- na⟩ dem Soh- ne Da- vid!
Vne.
B.c.
4 ♯ ♯
30
FAV.
T
sie- he, dein Kö- nig, dein Kö- nig kommt zu dir sanfft- mü- tig und rei- tet auff
Vne.
B.c.
♯ ♯ 6 6 6

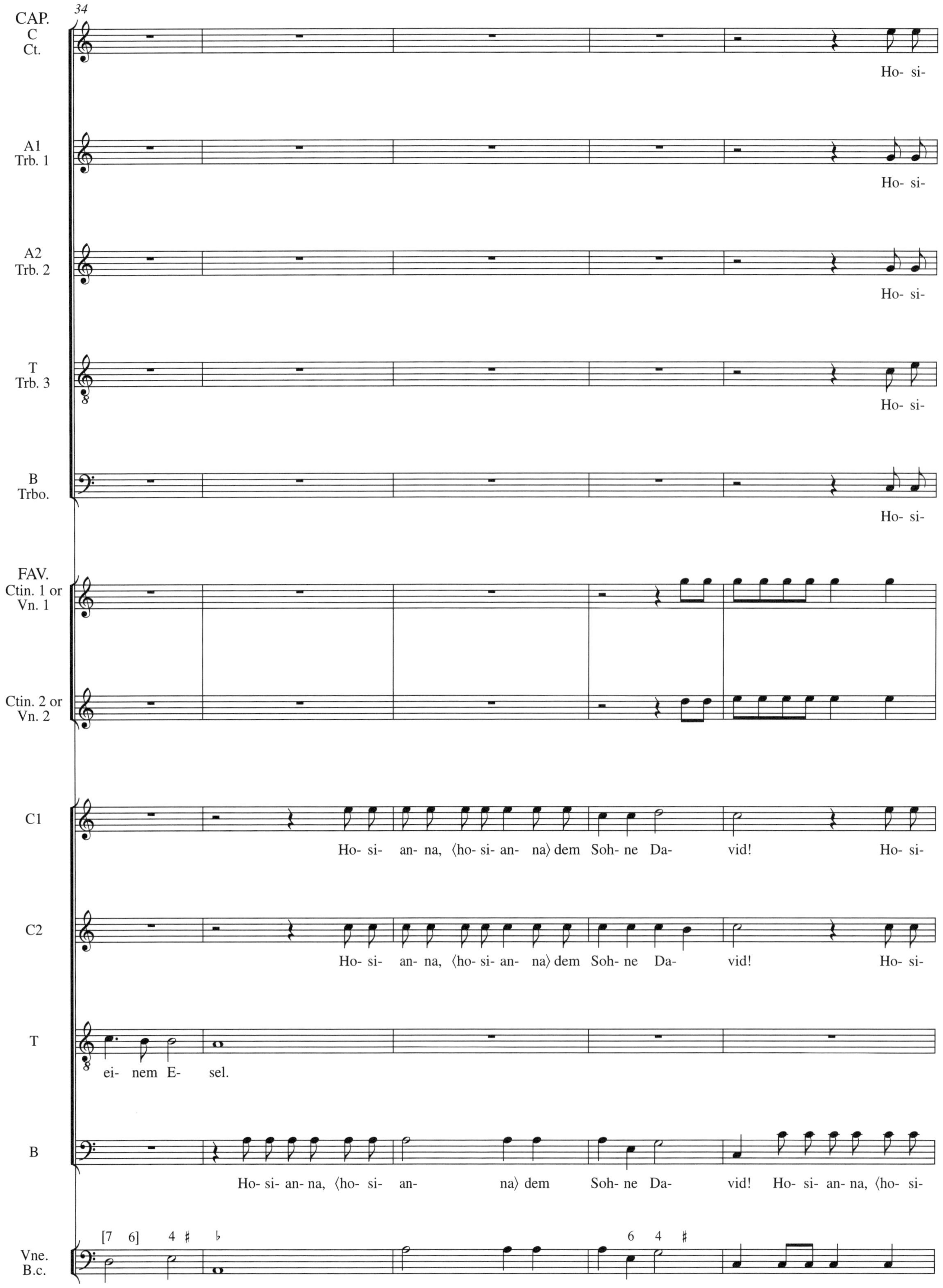

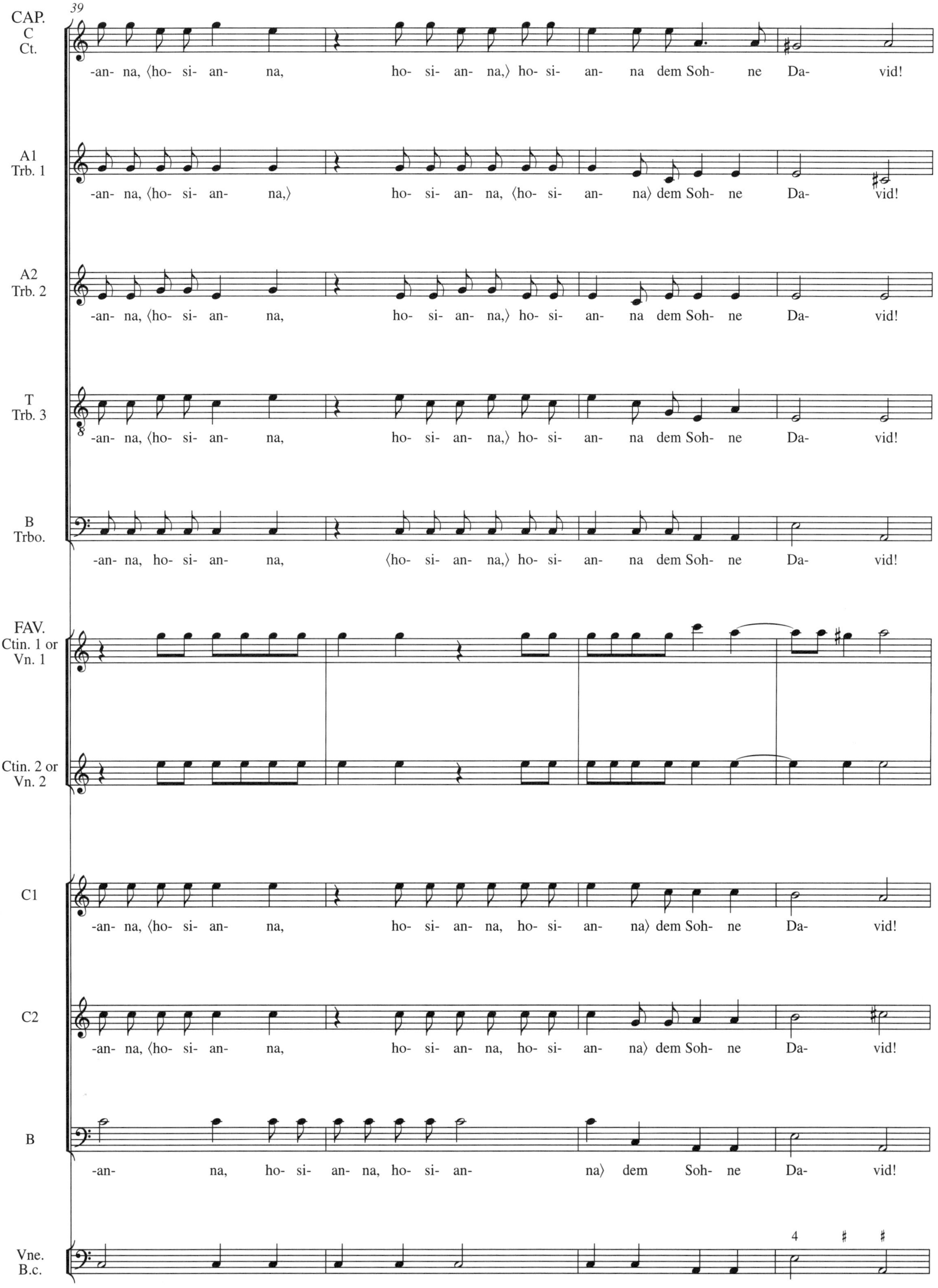

43
FAV.
C1
Ge- lo- bet sey, der da kommt in [Na]- - men des Her-
C2
Ge- lo- bet sey, der da kommt in Na- - men des Her-
B
Ge- lo- bet sey, der da kommt in Na- - men des Her- ren!
Vne.
B.c.
48
FAV.
C1
-ren! Ge- lo- bet sey, der da kommt in Na- - [men] des Her-
C2
-ren! Ge- lo- bet sey, der da kommt in Na- - men des Her-
B
Ge- lo- bet sey, der da kommt in Na- - men des Her- ren!
Vne.
B.c.
53
FAV.
C1
-ren, in Na- men des Her- ren!
C2
-ren, in Na- men des Her- ren!
T
Freu- e dich, du Toch- ter
B
Ge- lo- bet sey, der da kommt in Na- - men des Her- ren!
Vne.
B.c.

58
FAV.
Ctin. 1 or Vn. 1
Ctin. 2 or Vn. 2
T
Zi- on, ⟨freu- e dich, du Toch- ter Zi- on,⟩
Vne. B.c.
64
FAV.
Ctin. 1 or Vn. 1
Ctin. 2 or Vn. 2
T
und du, Toch- ter Je- ru- sa- lem, jauch-
Vne. B.c.
69
FAV.
Ctin. 1 or Vn. 1
Ctin. 2 or Vn. 2
T
- ze, jauch- ze, jauch- ze! Sie- he, dein Kö- nig kommt zu
Vne. B.c.

73
CAP.
C
Ct.
Ge- lo- bet sey, der da kommt,
A1
Trb. 1
Ge- lo- bet sey, der da kommt,
A2
Trb. 2
Ge- lo- bet sey, der da kommt,
T
Trb. 3
Ge- lo- bet sey, der da kommt,
B
Trbo.
Ge- lo- bet sey, der da kommt,
FAV.
Ctin. 1 or
Vn. 1
Ctin. 2 or
Vn. 2
C1
[Ge- lo- bet sey, der da kommt,]
C2
Ge- lo- bet sey, der da kommt,
T
dir sanfft- mü- tig, ⟨sie- he, dein Kö- nig kommt zu dir sanfft- mü-
B
Ge- lo- bet sey, der da kommt,
Vne.
B.c.
6 [♯]6 ♯ ♭ ♯ ♯ ♯ 6 4 ♯

77
CAP.
C
Ct.
ge- lo- bet sey, der da kommt,
⟨ge- lo- bet sey, der da
A1
Trb. 1
ge- lo- bet sey, der da kommt,
ge- lo- bet sey, der da
A2
Trb. 2
ge- lo- bet sey, der da kommt,
⟨ge- lo- bet sey, der da
T
Trb. 3
ge- lo- bet sey, der da kommt,
⟨ge- lo- bet sey, der da
B
Trbo.
ge- lo- bet sey, der da kommt,
⟨ge- lo- bet sey, der da
FAV.
Ctin. 1 or
Vn. 1
Ctin. 2 or
Vn. 2
C1
⟨ge- lo- bet sey, der da kommt,
ge- lo- bet sey, der da
C2
⟨ge- lo- bet sey, der da kommt,
ge- lo- bet sey, der da
T
-tig,
sie- he, dein Kö- nig kommt zu dir sanfft- mü- tig⟩
B
⟨ge- lo- bet sey, der da kommt,
ge- lo- bet sey, der da
Vne.
B.c.

81
CAP.
C
Ct.
kommt,〉 ge- lo- bet sey, der da kommt in
A1
Trb. 1
kommt, 〈ge- lo- bet sey, der da kommt〉 in
A2
Trb. 2
kommt, ge- lo- bet sey, der da kommt〉 in
T
Trb. 3
kommt,〉 ge- lo- bet sey, der da kommt in
B
Trbo.
kommt,〉 ge- lo- bet sey, der da kommt in
FAV.
Ctin. 1 or
Vn. 1
Ctin. 2 or
Vn. 2
C1
kommt, ge- lo- bet sey, der da kommt〉 in
C2
kommt, ge- lo- bet sey, der da kommt〉 in
T
und rei- - tet auff ei- nem E- sel.
B
kommt,〉 ge- lo- bet sey, der da kommt in
Vne.
B.c.

85
CAP.
C
Ct.
Na- men des Her- ren!
A1
Trb. 1
Na- men des Her- ren!
A2
Trb. 2
Na- men des Her- ren!
T
Trb. 3
Na- men des Her- ren!
B
Trbo.
Na- men des Her- ren!
FAV.
Ctin. 1 or
Vn. 1
Ctin. 2 or
Vn. 2
C1
Na- men des Her- ren! Ho- si- an- na in der Hö- he! Ho- si- an- na in der Hö-
C2
Na- men des Her- ren! Ho- si- an- na in der Hö- he! ⟨Ho- si- an- na in der Hö-
T
Ho- si- an- na in der Hö- he! Ho- si-
B
Na- men des Her- ren! Ho- si- an- na in der Hö- he! Ho- si- an- na in der Hö-
Vne.
B.c.

89
CAP.
C
Ct.
Ho- si- an- na, ⟨ho- si- an- na⟩ in der Hö- he!
A1
Trb. 1
Ho- si- an- na, ⟨ho- si- an- na⟩ in der Hö- he!
A2
Trb. 2
Ho- si- an- na, ⟨ho- si- an- na⟩ in der Hö- he!
T
Trb. 3
Ho- si- an- na, ⟨ho- si- an- na⟩ in der Hö- he!
B
Trbo.
Ho- si- an- na, ho- si- an- na in der Hö- he!
FAV.
Ctin. 1 or
Vn. 1
Ctin. 2 or
Vn. 2
C1
-he! ⟨Ho- si- an- na in der Hö- he!⟩ Ho- si- an- na, ⟨ho- si- an- na⟩ in der Hö- he!
C2
-he! Ho- si- an- na in der Hö- he!⟩ Ho- si- an- na, ⟨ho- si- an- na⟩ in der Hö- he!
T
-an- na in der Hö- he! ⟨Ho- si- an- na in der Hö- he!⟩ Ho- si- an- na, ⟨ho- si- an- na⟩ in der Hö- he!
B
-he! ⟨Ho- si- an- na in der Hö- he!⟩ Ho- si- an- na, ⟨ho- si- an- na⟩ in der Hö- he!
Vne.
B.c.

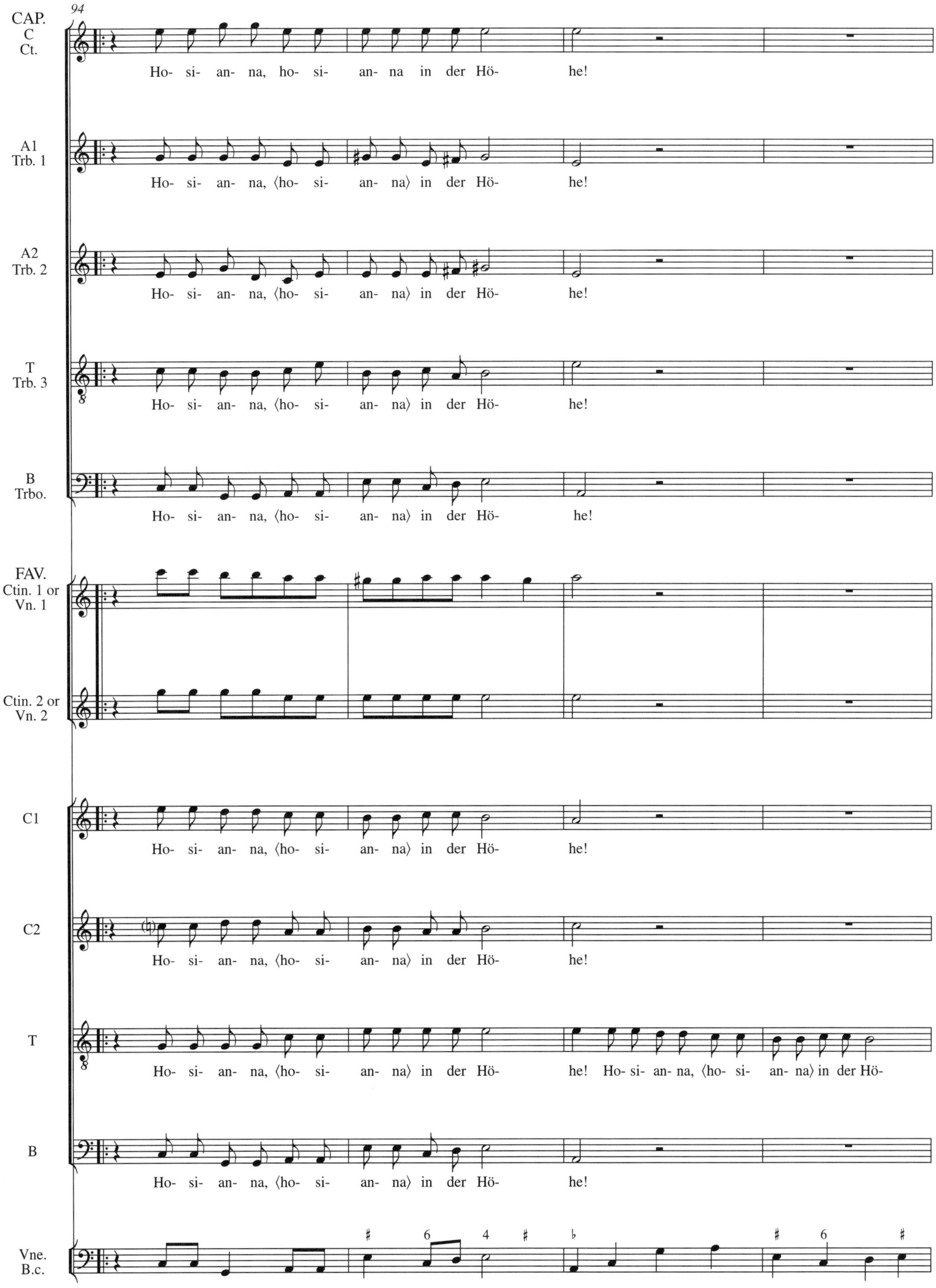

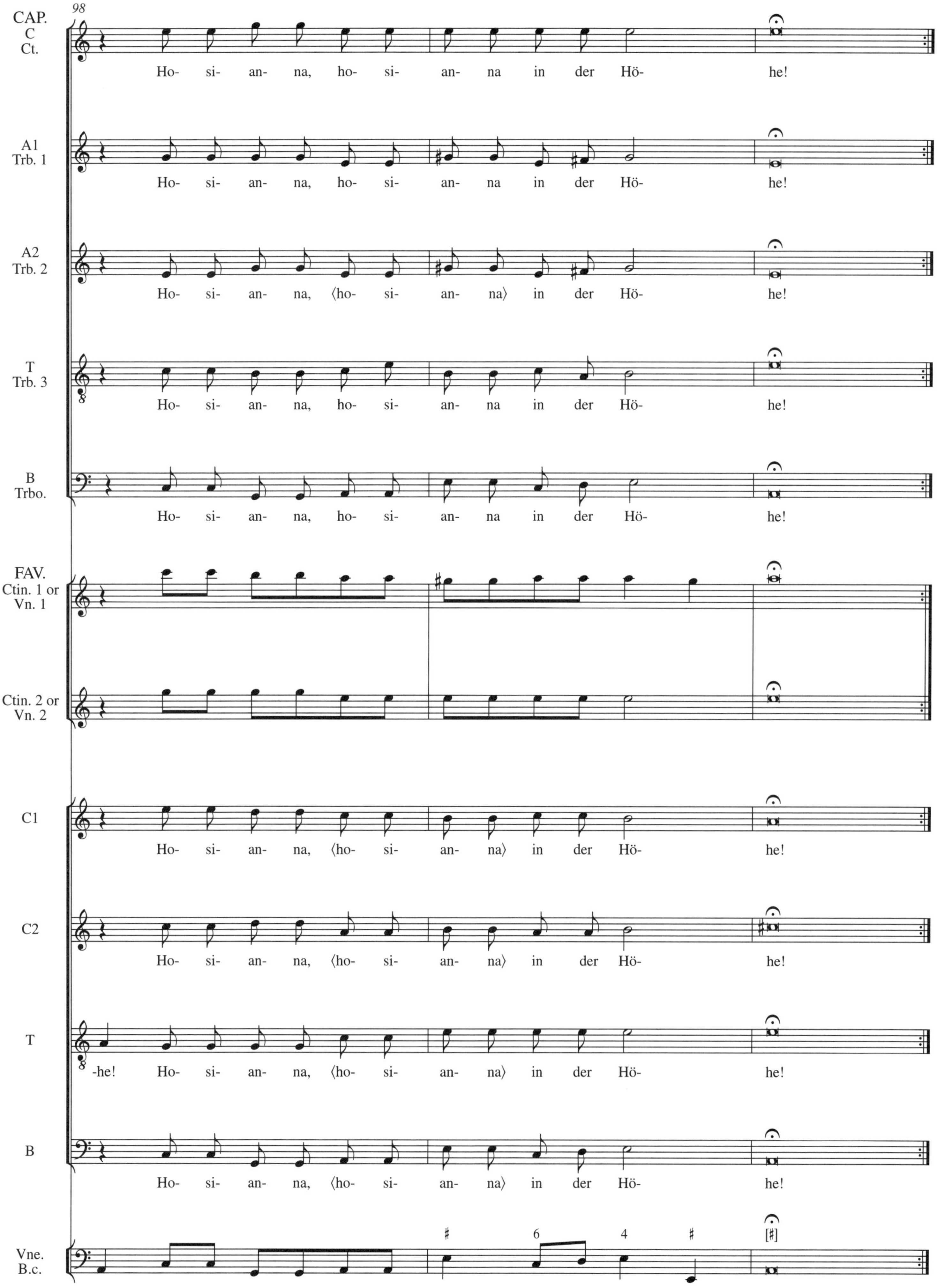

Mein Sohn, warumb hast du uns das gethan?

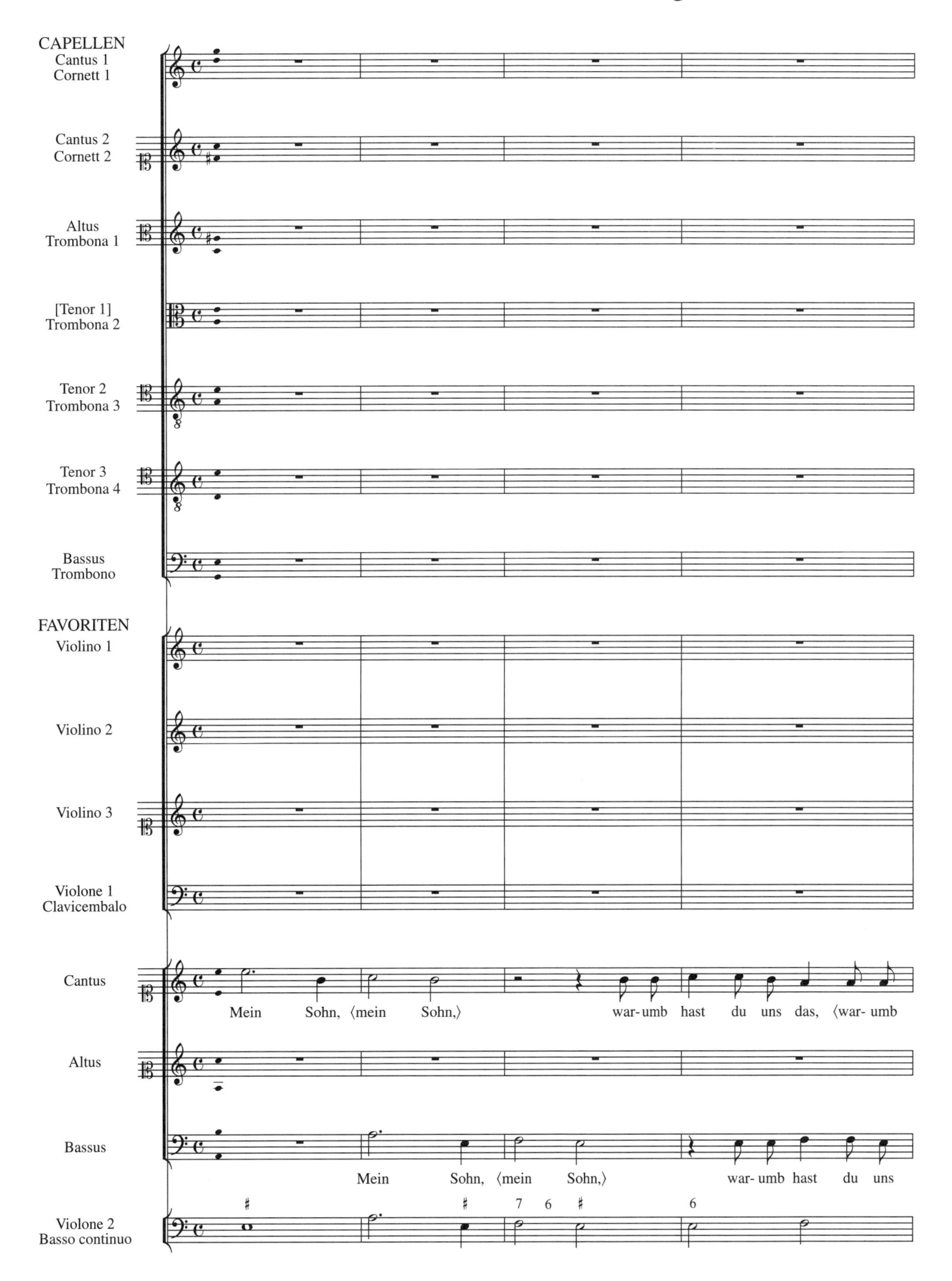

FAV.
C
B
Vne. 2
B.c.
hast du uns das⟩ ge- than? War-umb hast du uns das, ⟨war- umb hast du uns das, war-umb
das ge- than? Je mein Sohn, je mein Sohn, mein Sohn, ⟨mein
hast du uns das⟩ ge- than? Je mein Sohn, ⟨je mein Sohn,⟩ je
Sohn,⟩ mein Sohn, war- umb hast du uns das, war- umb hast du uns das,
mein Sohn, war- umb hast du uns das ge- than? Und ich, und
⟨war- umb hast du uns das⟩ ge- than? Sie- he, dein Va- ter, dein Va- ter,
ich, ⟨und ich, und ich⟩ ha- ben dich mit Schmer- - tzen ge-
⟨dein Va- ter⟩ ha- ben dich mit Schmer- - tzen ge-
A
-sucht.
Was ists, ⟨was ists,⟩ daß ihr mich ge- sucht habt, ⟨daß ihr mich ge- sucht habt?⟩ Was
-sucht.

19

20

21

22

23

24

25

26

109
CAP.
C1 Ct. 1
⟨Al- le- lu- ja, al- le- lu- ja, al- le- lu-
C2 Ct. 2
Al- le- lu- ja, ⟨al- le- lu- ja, al- le- lu-
A Trb. 1
Al- le- lu- ja, al- le- lu- ja,⟩ al- le- lu-
[T1] Trb. 2
Al- le- lu- ja, al- le- lu- ja, al- le- lu-
T2 Trb. 3
Al- le- lu- ja, al- le- lu- ja, al- le- lu-
T3 Trb. 4
Al- le- lu- ja, al- le- lu- ja,⟩ al- le- lu-
B Trbo.
⟨Al- le- lu- ja, al- le- lu- ja, al- le- lu-
FAV.
Vn. 1
Vn. 2
Vn. 3
Vne. 1 Clav.
C
Al- le- lu- ja, al- le- lu- ja, al- le- lu- ja, al- le- lu- ja, al- le- lu-
A
Al- le- lu- ja, al- le- lu- ja, al- le- lu-
B
Al- le- lu- ja, al- le- lu- ja, al- le- lu- ja, al- le- lu- ja, al- le- lu-
Vne. 2 B.c.

113
CAP.
C1 Ct. 1
-ja! Al- le- lu- ja, al- le- lu- ja,⟩ al- le- lu- ja, ⟨al- le-
C2 Ct. 2
-ja!⟩ Al- le- lu- ja, ⟨al- le- lu- ja, al- le- lu- ja, al- le-
A Trb. 1
-ja! Al- le- lu- ja, ⟨al- le- lu- ja, al- le- lu- ja, al- le-
[T1] Trb. 2
-ja! ⟨Al- le- lu- ja, al- le- lu- ja, al- le- lu- ja, al- le-
T2 Trb. 3
-ja!⟩ Al- le- lu- ja, al- le- lu- ja, ⟨al- le- lu- ja, al- le-
T3 Trb. 4
-ja! Al- le- lu- ja, ⟨al- le- lu- ja, al- le- lu- ja, al- le-
B Trbo.
-ja! Al- le- lu- ja,⟩ al- le- lu- ja, ⟨al- le- lu- ja, al- le-
FAV.
Vn. 1
Vn. 2
Vn. 3
Vne. 1 Clav.
C
-ja! Al- le- lu- ja, al- le- lu- ja,
A
-ja! Al- le- lu- ja, al- le- lu- ja, al- le- lu- ja, al- le-
B
-ja!⟩ Al- le- lu- ja, ⟨al- le- lu- ja,
Vne. 2 B.c.

117
CAP.
C1 Ct. 1
-lu- ja, al- le- lu- ja! Al- - le- lu- ja!〉
C2 Ct. 2
-lu- ja, al- le- lu- ja! Al- - le- lu- ja!〉
A Trb. 1
-lu- ja,〉 al- le- lu- ja! Al- le- lu- ja!
[T1] Trb. 2
-lu- ja,〉 al- le- lu- ja! Al- - le- lu- ja!
T2 Trb. 3
-lu- ja,〉 al- le- lu- ja! 〈Al- - le- lu- ja!〉
T3 Trb. 4
-lu- ja, al- le- lu- ja!〉 Al- le- lu- ja!
B Trbo.
-lu- ja, al- le- lu- ja! Al- - le- lu- ja!〉
FAV.
Vn. 1
Vn. 2
Vn. 3
Vne. 1 Clav.
C
al- le- lu- ja, al- le- lu- ja, al- le- lu- ja!〉 Al- - le- lu- ja!
A
-lu- ja, al- le- lu- ja!〉 Al- - le- lu- ja!
B
al- le- lu- ja, al- le- lu- ja, al- le- lu- ja!〉 Al- - le- lu- ja!
Vne. 2 B.c.

Herr, ich bin nicht werth

CAP.
Bom.
FAV.
Trb. 1
Trb. 2
T
Vne.
B.c.
Herr, ich bin nicht
werth, daß du un- ter mein Dach ein- ge- hest, ich bin nicht werth, Herr, ich bin nicht
werth, daß du un- ter mein Dach ein- ge- hest; sprich nur ein Wort, ⟨sprich nur ein
Wort, sprich nur ein Wort,⟩ so wird mei- ne See- le ge- sund, nur ein Wort, so
wird mei- ne See- le ge- sund.
B
Ich bin der Herr, ich bin der Herr, dein Artzt, ich bin der

26
CAP.
Bom.
FAV.
Trb. 1
Trb. 2
B
Herr, ich bin der Herr, dein Artzt, ich bin der Herr, ⟨ich bin der
Vne.
B.c.
30
CAP.
Bom.
FAV.
Trb. 1
Trb. 2
C1
Herr, ich bin nicht werth, daß du un- ter mein Dach ein- ge-
C2
Herr, ich bin nicht werth, daß du un- ter mein Dach ein- ge-
B
Herr,⟩ dein Artzt.
Vne.
B.c.
34
FAV.
C1
-hest, ich bin nicht werth, Herr, ich bin nicht werth, daß du un- ter mein Dach ein- ge-
C2
-hest, ich bin nicht werth, Herr, ich bin nicht werth, daß du un- ter mein Dach ein- ge-
Vne.
B.c.

33

-hest; sprich nur ein Wort, ⟨sprich nur ein Wort, sprich nur ein

-hest; sprich nur ein Wort, ⟨sprich nur ein Wort, sprich nur ein Wort, sprich nur ein

Wort,⟩ so wird mei- ne See- le ge- sund, nur ein Wort, so wird mei- ne See- le ge-

Wort,⟩ so wird mei- ne See- le ge- sund, nur ein Wort, so wird mei- ne See- le ge-

-sund.

-sund.

Ich bin der Herr, ich bin der Herr, dein Artzt, ich bin der

49
CAP.
Bom.
FAV.
Trb. 1
Trb. 2
T
Sprich nur ein Wort, nur ein Wort, so
B
Herr, ⟨ich bin der Herr,⟩ dein Artzt.
Vne.
B.c.
[6]
4
53
wird mei- ne See- le ge- sund, nur ein Wort, sprich nur ein Wort,
Sey ge-trost, sey ge- trost; dei- ne Sün- de
6

35

65
FAV.
C1
-sund, ⟨sprich nur ein Wort, so wird mei- ne See- le ge- sund,⟩ sprich nur
C2
-sund, ⟨sprich nur ein Wort, so wird mei- ne See- le ge- sund,⟩
T
ein Wort, ⟨sprich nur ein Wort,
B
Sey ge- trost, sey ge-
Vne.
B.c.
6 ♯ ♯
69
CAP.
Bom.
FAV.
Trb. 1
Trb. 2
C1
ein Wort, ⟨sprich nur ein Wort,⟩ so
C2
sprich nur ein Wort, ⟨sprich nur ein Wort,⟩ so
T
sprich nur ein Wort,⟩ so
B
-trost, ⟨sey ge- trost, sey ge- trost;⟩
Vne.
B.c.
♯ ♯ ♯ ♯

73
CAP.
Bom.
FAV.
Trb. 1
Trb. 2
C1
wird mei- ne See- le ge- sund.
C2
wird mei- ne See- le ge- sund.
T
wird mei- ne See- le ge- sund.
B
dei- ne Sün- de sind dir ver- ge- ben,
Vne.
B.c.

77
CAP.
Bom.
FAV.
Trb. 1
Trb. 2
B
⟨dei- ne Sün- de sind dir ver- ge- ben.⟩ Ge- he hin; dir ge- sche- he, wie du, wie du ge-
Vne.
B.c.

38

85
CAP.
C1 Ct. 1
Her- ren, lo- be den Her- ren, lo- be den Her- ren, und
C2 Ct. 2
Her- ren, lo- be den Her- ren, lo- be den Her- ren, und
A Trb. 1
Her- ren, lo- be den Her- ren, lo- be den Her- ren, und
T1 Trb. 2
Her- ren, lo- be den Her- ren, lo- be den Her- ren, und
T2 Trb. 3
Her- ren, ⟨lo- be den Her- ren,⟩ lo- be den Her- ren, und
B Bom.
Her- ren, lo- be den Her- ren, ⟨lo- be den Her- ren,⟩ und
FAV.
Trb. 1
Trb. 2
C1
Her- ren, mei- ne See- le, lo- be den Her- ren, lo- be den Her- ren, und
C2
Her- ren, ⟨mei- ne See- le, lo- be den Her- ren,⟩ lo- be den Her- ren, und
T
Her- ren, ⟨lo- be den Her- ren,⟩ mei- ne See- le, lo- be den Her- ren, und
B
Her- ren, ⟨lo- be den Her- ren, lo- be den Her- ren,⟩ und
Vne. B.c.

89
CAP.
C1 Ct. 1
— ver- giß nicht, was er dir Guts, ge- than
C2 Ct. 2
— ver- giß nicht, was er dir Guts ge- than
A Trb. 1
— ver- giß nicht, was er dir Guts ge- than
T1 Trb. 2
— ver- giß nicht, was er dir Guts ge- than
T2 Trb. 3
— ver- giß nicht, was er dir Guts ge- than
B Bom.
— ver- giß nicht, was er dir Guts ge- than
FAV.
Trb. 1
Trb. 2
C1
— ver- giß nicht, was er dir Guts ge- than
C2
— ver- giß nicht, was er dir Guts ge- than
T
— ver- giß nicht, was er dir Guts ge- than
B
— ver- giß nicht, was er dir Guts ge- than
Vne. B.c.
♭ ♯ ♭ 4 ♯

41

97
CAP.
C1
Ct. 1
Guts ge- than hat.
C2
Ct. 2
Guts ge- than hat.
A
Trb. 1
Guts ge- than hat.
T1
Trb. 2
Guts ge- than hat.
T2
Trb. 3
Guts ge- than hat.
B
Bom.
Guts ge- than hat.
FAV.
Trb. 1
Trb. 2
C1
Guts ge- than hat: der dir al- le dei- ne Sün- de ver-
C2
Guts ge- than hat: der dir al- le dei- ne Sün- de ver-
T
Guts ge- than hat:
B
Guts ge- than hat: lo- be,
Vne.
B.c.

101
FAV.
Trb. 1
Trb. 2
C1
-gie- bet, ⟨der dir al- le dei- ne Sün- de ver- gie-
C2
-gie- bet, ⟨der dir al- le dei- ne Sün- de ver- gie-
T
der dir al- le dei- ne Sün- de ver- gie- bet,
B
lo- be den Herrn, lo- be, lo- be den Herrn, ⟨lo- be, lo- be den
Vne.
B.c.
105
FAV.
Trb. 1
Trb. 2
C1
-bet⟩ und hei- let al- le dei- ne Ge- bre- chen.
C2
-bet⟩ und hei- let al- le dei- ne Ge- bre- chen.
T
⟨der dir al- le dei- ne- Sün- de ver- gie- bet⟩ und hei- let al- le
B
Herrn, lo- be, lo- be den Herrn, lo- be, lo- be den Herrn,
Vne.
B.c.

109
CAP.
C1 Ct. 1
Lo- be den Her- ren, lo- be den Her- ren,
C2 Ct. 2
Lo- be den Her- ren, lo- be den Her- ren,
A Trb. 1
Lo- be den Her- ren, lo- be den Her- ren,
T1 Trb. 2
Lo- be den Her- ren, lo- be den Her- ren,
T2 Trb. 3
Lo- be den Her- ren, lo- be den Her- ren,
B Bom.
Lo- be den Her- ren, lo- be den Her- ren,
FAV.
Trb. 1
Trb. 2
C1
Mei- ne See- le, lo- be den Her- ren, ⟨mei- ne See- le, lo- be den Her- ren,⟩
C2
Mei- ne See- le, lo- be den Her- ren, ⟨mei- ne See- le, lo- be den Her- ren,⟩
T
dei- ne Ge- bre- chen. Lo- be den Her- ren, ⟨lo- be den Her- ren,⟩
B
lo- be, lo- be den Herrn.⟩ Lo- be den Her- ren, ⟨lo- be den Her- ren,
Vne. B.c.

45

118
CAP.
C1 Ct. 1
-than hat, was er dir Guts, Guts,
C2 Ct. 2
-than hat, was er dir Guts, Guts,
A Trb. 1
-than hat, was er dir Guts, Guts,
T1 Trb. 2
-than hat, was er dir Guts, Guts,
T2 Trb. 3
-than hat, was er dir Guts, Guts,
B Bom.
[Bom.]
[Bom.]
-than hat, was er dir Guts, Guts,
FAV.
Trb. 1
Trb. 2
C1
-than hat, was er dir Guts, Guts,
C2
-than hat, was er dir Guts, Guts,
T
-than hat, was er dir Guts, Guts,
B
-than hat, was er dir Guts, Guts,
Vne. B.c.
4 ♯ ♯ ♭

47

127
CAP.
C1 Ct. 1
ge- than hat.
C2 Ct. 2
ge- than hat.
A Trb. 1
was er dir guts ge- than, ge- than hat.
T1 Trb. 2
ge- than hat.
T2 Trb. 3
ge- than hat.
B Bom.
ge- than hat.
FAV.
Trb. 1
Trb. 2
C1
ge- than hat.
C2
ge- than hat.
T
ge- than hat.
B
ge- than hat.
Vne. B.c.
[♯]

O Herr hilf, wir verderben!

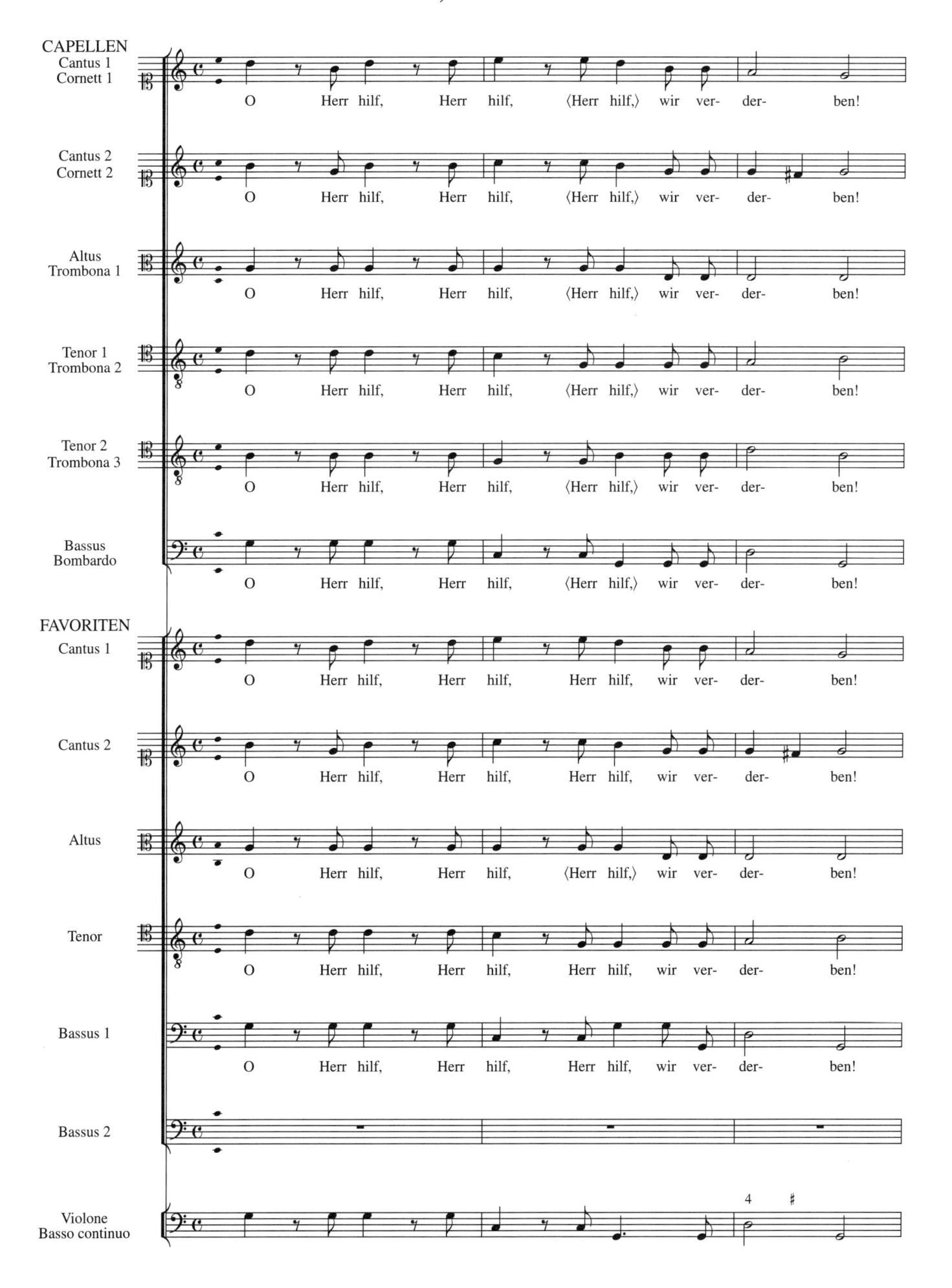

CAP.
C1 Ct. 1
O Herr hilf, wir ver- der- ben!
C2 Ct. 2
O Herr hilf, wir ver- der- ben!
A Trb. 1
O Herr hilf, wir ver- der- ben!
T1 Trb. 2
O Herr hilf, wir ver- der- ben!
T2 Trb. 3
O Herr hilf, wir ver- der- ben!
B Bom.
O Herr hilf, wir ver- der- ben!
FAV.
C1
Mei- ster, ⟨Mei- ster,⟩ wir ver- der- ben! Herr hilf, wir ver- der- ben!
C2
Mei- ster, Mei- ster, wir ver- der- ben! Herr hilf, wir ver- der- ben!
A
Mei- ster, ⟨Mei- ster,⟩ wir ver- der- ben! O Herr hilf, wir ver- der- ben!
T
Mei- ster, Mei- ster, wir ver- der- ben! O Herr hilf, wir ver- der- ben!
B1
Wir ver- der- ben! ⟨Wir ver- der- ben!⟩ Herr hilf, wir ver- der- ben!
Vne. B.c.
FAV.
A
Mei- ster, fragst du nichts dar- nach, wir ver- der- ben, fragst du nichts dar- nach, wir ver-
T
Mei- ster, fragst du nichts dar- nach, wir ver- der- ben, fragst du nichts dar- nach, wir ver-
B1
O Herr hilf, ⟨o Herr hilf, o Herr hilf,
Vne. B.c.

12
CAP.
C1 Ct. 1
Herr
C2 Ct. 2
Herr
A Trb. 1
Herr
T1 Trb. 2
Herr
T2 Trb. 3
Herr
B Bom.
Herr
FAV.
C1
Mei- ster, fragst du nichts dar- nach, wir ver- der- ben! O Herr
C2
Mei- ster, fragst du nichts dar- nach, wir ver- der- ben! O Herr
A
-der- ben! O Herr
T
-der- ben! O Herr
B1
o Herr hilf, o Herr hilf, o Herr hilf, o Herr hilf,〉 Herr
B2
Vne. B.c.

16
CAP.
C1
Ct. 1
hilf, wir ver- der- ben! O Herr hilf, ⟨Herr hilf,⟩
C2
Ct. 2
hilf, wir ver- der- ben! O Herr hilf, Herr hilf,
A
Trb. 1
hilf, wir ver- der- ben! O Herr hilf, Herr hilf,
T1
Trb. 2
hilf, wir ver- der- ben! O Herr hilf, Herr hilf,
T2
Trb. 3
hilf, wir ver- der- ben! O Herr hilf, Herr hilf,
B
Bom.
hilf, wir ver- der- ben! O Herr hilf, Herr hilf,
FAV.
C1
hilf, wir ver- der- ben! O Herr hilf, Herr hilf,
C2
hilf, wir ver- der- ben! O Herr hilf, Herr hilf,
A
hilf, wir ver- der- ben! O Herr hilf, Herr hilf,
T
hilf, wir ver- der- ben! O Herr hilf, Herr hilf,
B1
hilf, wir ver- der- ben! O Herr hilf, Herr hilf,
B2
O ihr Klein- gläu- bi- gen, ⟨o
Vne.
B.c.

20
CAP.
C1
Ct. 1
O Herr hilf, wir ver- der- ben!
C2
Ct. 2
O Herr hilf, wir ver- der- ben!
A
Trb. 1
O Herr hilf, wir ver- der- ben!
T1
Trb. 2
O Herr hilf, wir ver- der- ben!
T2
Trb. 3
O Herr hilf, wir ver- der- ben!
B
Bom.
O Herr hilf, wir ver- der- ben!
FAV.
C1
O Herr hilf, wir ver- der- ben!
C2
O Herr hilf, wir ver- der- ben!
A
O Herr hilf, wir ver- der- ben!
T
O Herr hilf, wir ver- der- ben!
B1
O Herr hilf, wir ver- der- ben!
B2
ihr Klein- gläu- bi- gen,〉 wo, wo ist eu- er Glau- be? O ihr Klein-
[6]
[6]
Vne.
B.c.

24
CAP.
C1
Ct. 1
O Herr hilf, ⟨Herr hilf,⟩ wir ver- der- ben!
C2
Ct. 2
O Herr hilf, Herr hilf, wir ver- der- ben!
A
Trb. 1
O Herr hilf, Herr hilf, wir ver- der- ben!
T1
Trb. 2
O Herr hilf, Herr hilf, wir ver- der- ben!
T2
Trb. 3
O Herr hilf, Herr hilf, wir ver- der- ben!
B
Bom.
O Herr hilf, Herr hilf, wir ver- der- ben!
FAV.
C1
O Herr hilf, Herr hilf, wir ver- der- ben!
C2
O Herr hilf, Herr hilf, wir ver- der- ben!
A
O Herr hilf, Herr hilf, wir ver- der- ben!
T
O Herr hilf, Herr hilf, wir ver- der- ben!
B1
O Herr hilf, Herr hilf, wir ver- der- ben!
B2
-gläu- bi- gen, ⟨o ihr Klein- gläu- bi-
Vne.
B.c.
4 ♯ ♯

28
CAP.
C1 Ct. 1
O Herr hilf, Herr hilf,
C2 Ct. 2
O Herr hilf, Herr hilf,
A Trb. 1
O Herr hilf, Herr hilf,
T1 Trb. 2
O Herr hilf, Herr hilf,
T2 Trb. 3
O Herr hilf, Herr hilf,
B Bom.
O Herr hilf, Herr hilf,
FAV.
C1
O Herr hilf, Herr hilf,
C2
O Herr hilf, Herr hilf,
A
O Herr hilf, Herr hilf,
T
O Herr hilf, Herr hilf,
B1
O Herr hilf, Herr hilf,
B2
-gen,〉 wo, wo ist eu- er Glau- be? O ihr Klein- gläu- bi- gen, 〈o
Vne. B.c.

32
CAP.
C1
Ct. 1
wir ver- der- ben! O Herr hilf, Herr
C2
Ct. 2
wir ver- der- ben! O Herr hilf, Herr
A
Trb. 1
wir ver- der- ben! O Herr hilf, Herr
T1
Trb. 2
wir ver- der- ben! O Herr hilf, Herr
T2
Trb. 3
wir ver- der- ben! O Herr hilf, Herr
B
Bom.
wir ver- der- ben! O Herr hilf, Herr
FAV.
C1
wir ver- der- ben! O Herr hilf, Herr
C2
wir ver- der- ben! O Herr hilf, Herr
A
wir ver- der- ben! O Herr hilf, Herr
T
wir ver- der- ben! O Herr hilf, Herr
B1
wir ver- der- ben! O Herr hilf, Herr
B2
ihr Klein- gläu- bi- gen, o ihr Klein- gläu- bi- gen,
Vne.
B.c.
6
6

36
CAP.
C1
Ct. 1
hilf, wir ver- der- ben! O Herr hilf, wir ver- der- ben,
C2
Ct. 2
hilf, wir ver- der- ben! O Herr hilf, wir ver- der- ben,
A
Trb. 1
hilf, wir ver- der- ben! O Herr hilf, wir ver- der- ben,
T1
Trb. 2
hilf, wir ver- der- ben! O Herr hilf, wir ver- der- ben,
T2
Trb. 3
hilf, wir ver- der- ben! O Herr hilf, wir ver- der- ben,
B
Bom.
hilf, wir ver- der- ben! O Herr hilf, wir ver- der- ben,
FAV.
C1
hilf, wir ver- der- ben! O Herr hilf, wir ver- der- ben,
C2
hilf, wir ver- der- ben! O Herr hilf, wir ver- der- ben,
A
hilf, wir ver- der- ben! O Herr hilf, wir ver- der- ben,
T
hilf, wir ver- der- ben! O Herr hilf, wir ver- der- ben,
B1
hilf, wir ver- der- ben! O Herr hilf, wir ver- der- ben,
B2
o ihr Klein- gläu- bi- gen, o ihr Klein-
Vne.
B.c.

40
CAP.
C1
Ct. 1
wir ver- der- ben! O Herr
C2
Ct. 2
wir ver- der- ben! O Herr
A
Trb. 1
wir ver- der- ben! O Herr
T1
Trb. 2
wir ver- der- ben! O Herr
T2
Trb. 3
wir ver- der- ben! O Herr
B
Bom.
wir ver- der- ben! O Herr
FAV.
C1
wir ver- der- ben! O Herr
C2
wir ver- der- ben! O Herr
A
wir ver- der- ben! O Herr
T
wir ver- der- ben! O Herr
B1
⟨wir ver- der- ben!⟩ O Herr
B2
-gläu- bi- gen,⟩ wo, wo ist eu- er Glau- be? O ihr Klein- gläu- bi- gen,
Vne.
B.c.
[6]

59

60

61

56
CAP.
C1
Ct. 1
[O Herr hilf, wir ver-
C2
Ct. 2
O Herr hilf, wir ver-
A
Trb. 1
O Herr hilf, wir ver-
T1
Trb. 2
O Herr hilf, wir ver-
T2
Trb. 3
O Herr hilf, wir ver-
B
Bom.
O Herr hilf, wir ver-
FAV.
C1
Mei- ster, fragst du nichts dar-nach, wir ver-der- ben! Herr hilf, wir ver-
C2
Mei- ster, fragst du nichts dar-nach, wir ver- der- ben! Herr hilf, wir ver-
A
-der- ben, fragst du nichts dar- nach! O Herr hilf, wir ver-
T
-der- ben, fragst du nichts dar- nach! O Herr hilf, wir ver-
B1
hilf, o Herr hilf, o Herr hilf, o Herr hilf,〉 Herr hilf, wir ver-
B2
Vne.
B.c.
[4 3]

60
CAP.
C1
Ct. 1
-der- ben! O Herr hilf, Herr
C2
Ct. 2
-der- ben! O Herr hilf, Herr
A
Trb. 1
-der- ben! O Herr hilf, Herr
T1
Trb. 2
-der- ben! O Herr hilf, Herr
T2
Trb. 3
-der- ben! O Herr hilf, Herr
B
Bom.
-der- ben! O Herr hilf, Herr
FAV.
C1
-der- ben! O Herr hilf, Herr
C2
-der- ben! O Herr hilf, Herr
A
-der- ben! O Herr hilf, Herr
T
-der- ben! O Herr hilf, Herr
B1
-der- ben! O Herr hilf, Herr
B2
⟨o ihr Klein- gläu- bi- gen,⟩ wo, wo ist eu- er Glau- be?
Vne.
B.c.

64

68
CAP.
C1
Ct. 1
wir ver- der- ben!
C2
Ct. 2
hilf, wir ver- der- ben!
A
Trb. 1
-der- - ben!
T1
Trb. 2
hilf,⟩ wir ver- der- ben!
T2
Trb. 3
hilf,⟩ wir ver- der- ben!
B
Bom.
-der- - ben!⟩
FAV.
C1
wir ver- der- ben!
C2
hilf, wir ver- der- ben!
A
-der- - ben!
T
hilf,⟩ wir ver- der- ben!
B1
-der- - ben!
B2
Wind und Meer schweig, schweig und ver-stum-me, schweig,
[7 6]
4
Vne.
B.c.

73
FAV.
B2
⟨schweig⟩ und ver- stum- me! Wind und Meer schweig, ⟨schweig⟩ und ver- stum- me, schweig,
Vne.
B.c.
76
CAP.
C1
Ct. 1
Was ist das für ein Mann, für ein Mann,
C2
Ct. 2
Was ist das für ein Mann, für ein Mann,
A
Trb. 1
Was ist das für ein Mann, was ist das für ein Mann, für ein Mann,
T1
Trb. 2
Was ist das für ein Mann, ⟨was ist das für ein Mann,⟩ für ein Mann,
T2
Trb. 3
Was ist das für ein Mann, ⟨was ist das für ein Mann,⟩ für ein Mann,
B
Bom.
Was ist das für ein Mann, ⟨was ist das für ein Mann,⟩ für ein Mann,
FAV.
C1
Was ist das für ein Mann, für ein Mann, dem Wind und Meer
C2
Was ist das für ein Mann, für ein Mann, dem Wind und Meer
A
Was ist das für ein Mann, ⟨was ist das für ein Mann,⟩ für ein Mann,
T
Was ist das für ein Mann, ⟨was ist das für ein Mann,⟩ für ein Mann,
B1
Was ist das für ein Mann, ⟨was ist das für ein Mann,⟩ für ein Mann, dem Wind und
B2
⟨schweig⟩ und ver-stum- me!
Vne.
B.c.

67

68

92
CAP.
C1 Ct. 1
Mann, dem Wind und_ Meer, dem Wind und_ Meer ge- hor- sam
C2 Ct. 2
Mann, dem Wind und_ Meer, dem Wind und_ Meer ge- hor- sam
A Trb. 1
Mann,〉 dem Wind und Meer ge- hor- sam
T1 Trb. 2
Mann,〉 dem Wind und_ Meer ge- hor- sam
T2 Trb. 3
Mann,〉 dem___ Wind und_ Meer ge- hor- sam
B Bom.
Mann, dem Wind und_ Meer ge- hor- sam
FAV.
C1
Mann,〉 dem Wind und_ Meer, dem Wind und_ Meer ge- hor- sam
C2
Mann,〉 dem Wind und_ Meer, dem Wind und_ Meer ge- hor- sam
A
Mann,〉 dem Wind und_ Meer, dem Wind und Meer ge- hor- sam
T
Mann,〉 dem Wind und_ Meer, dem Wind und_ Meer ge- hor- sam
B1
Mann,〉 dem Wind und_ Meer, dem Wind und_ Meer ge- hor- sam
B2
Vne. B.c.
[6]

96
Presto
CAP.
C1
Ct. 1
ist? Al- le- lu- ja, al- le- lu- ja!
C2
Ct. 2
ist? Al- le- lu- ja, ⟨al- le- lu- ja!
A
Trb. 1
ist? Al- le- lu- ja, ⟨al- le- lu- ja!
T1
Trb. 2
ist? Al- le- lu- ja, ⟨al- le- lu- ja!⟩
T2
Trb. 3
ist? Al- le- lu- ja, ⟨al- le- lu- ja!
B
Bom.
ist? Al- le- lu- ja, al- le- lu- ja!
FAV.
Presto
C1
ist? Al- le- lu- ja, ⟨al- le- lu- ja!
C2
ist? Al- le- lu- ja, ⟨al- le- lu- ja!
A
ist? Al- le- lu- ja, ⟨al- le- lu- ja!
T
ist? Al- le- lu- ja, ⟨al- le- lu- ja!
B1
ist? Al- le- lu- ja, ⟨al- le- lu- ja!
B2
Al- le- lu- ja, ⟨al- le- lu- ja!⟩
Vne.
B.c.

101
CAP.
C1
Ct. 1
Al- le- lu- ja, al- le- lu- ja, al- le- lu- ja,
C2
Ct. 2
Al- le- lu- ja, al- le- lu- ja, al- le- lu- ja,⟩
A
Trb. 1
Al- le- lu- ja,⟩ al- le- lu- ja, ⟨al- le- lu- ja,
T1
Trb. 2
Al- le- lu- ja, ⟨al- le- lu- ja, al- le- lu- ja,
T2
Trb. 3
Al- le- lu- ja, al- le- lu- ja, al- le- lu- ja,⟩
B
Bom.
Al- le- lu- ja, ⟨al- le- lu- ja, al- le- lu- ja,
FAV.
C1
Al- le- lu- ja, al- le- lu- ja, al- le- lu- ja,
C2
Al- le- lu- ja, al- le- lu- ja, al- le- lu- ja,
A
Al- le- lu- ja, al- le- lu- ja, al- le- lu- ja,
T
Al- le- lu- ja, al- le- lu- ja, al- le- lu- ja,
B1
Al- le- lu- ja, al- le- lu- ja, al- le- lu- ja,⟩
B2
Al- le- lu- ja, ⟨al- le- lu- ja!
Vne.
B.c.
6 ♯ ♯ ♯

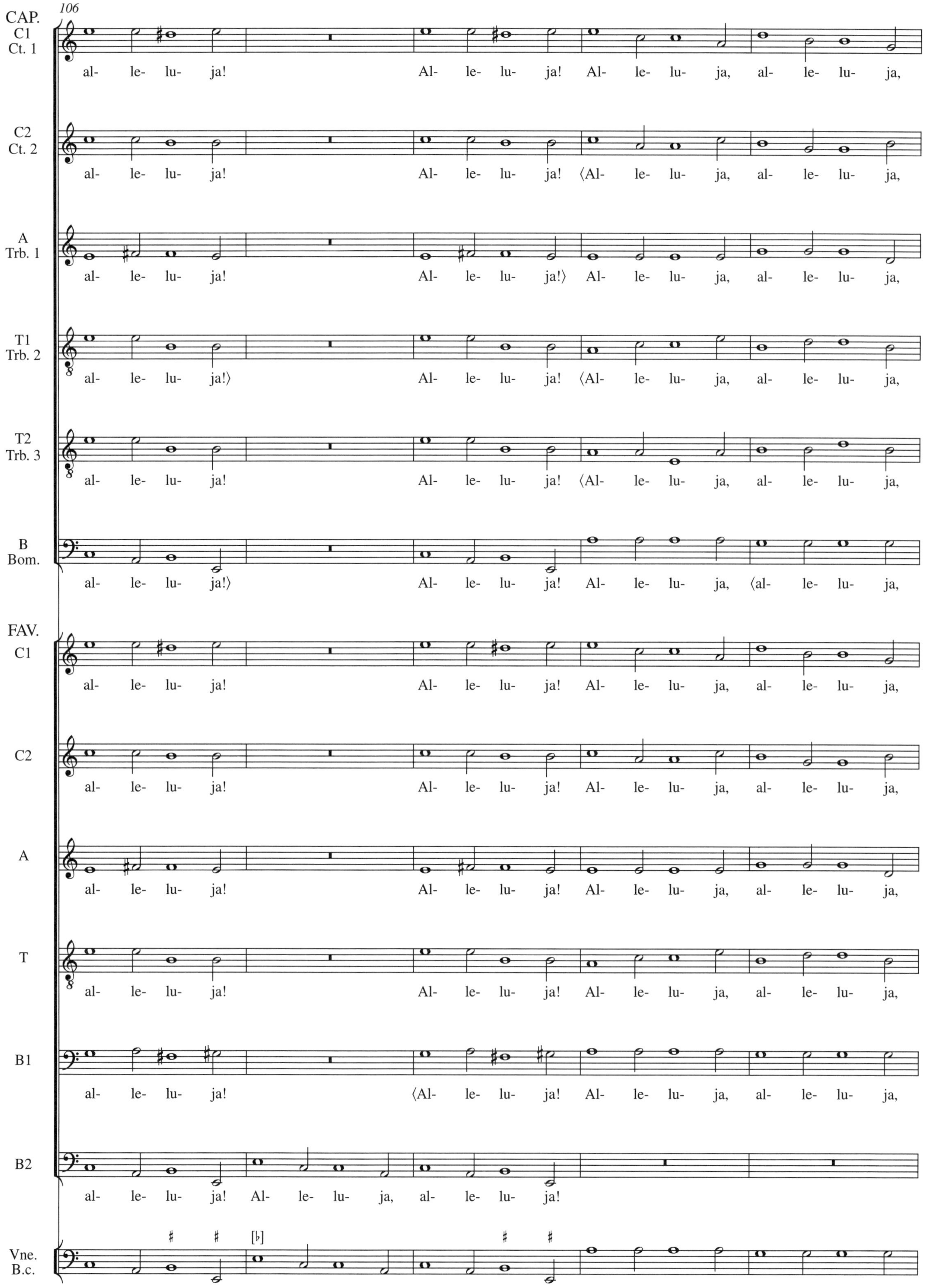

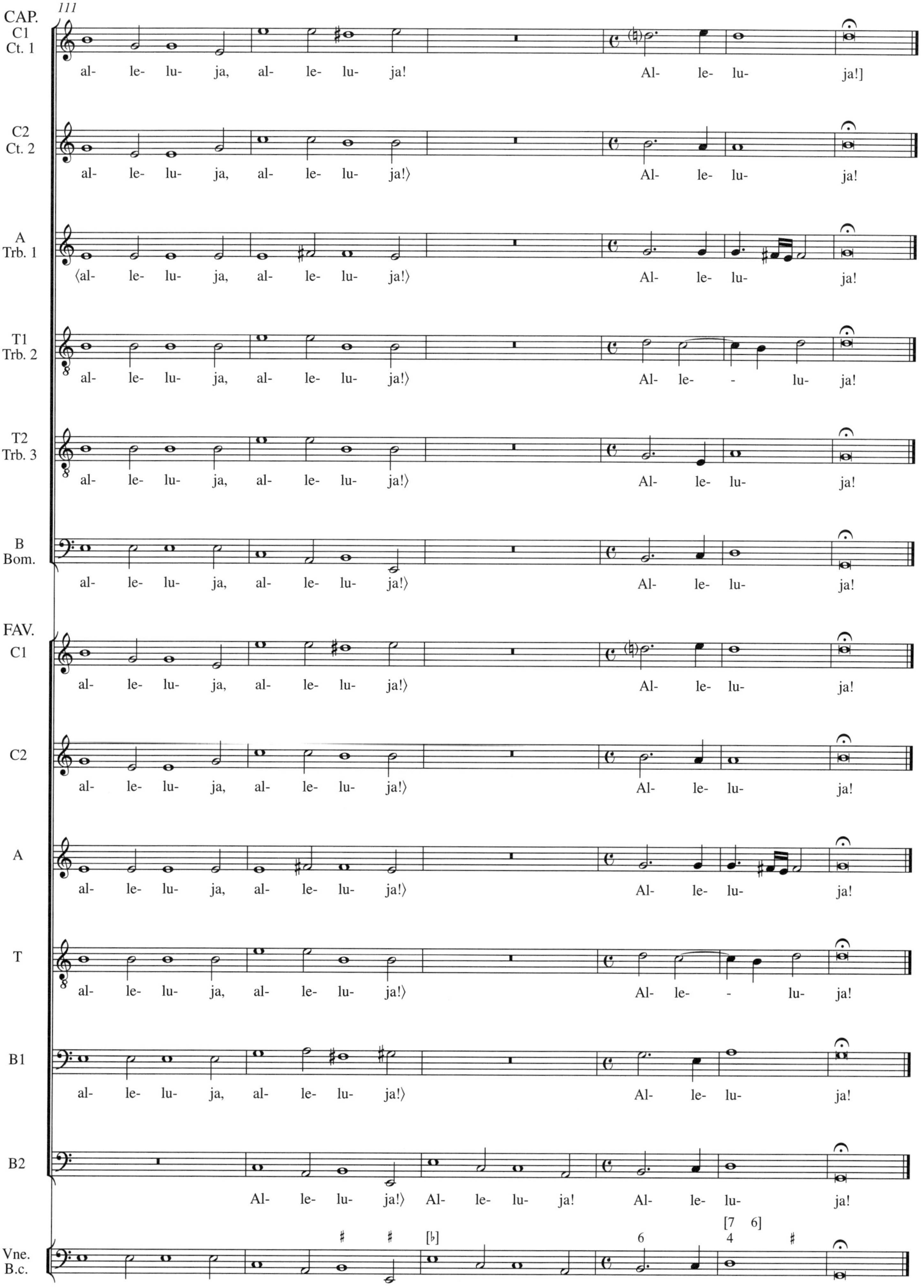

O Vater, aller Augen warten auff dich

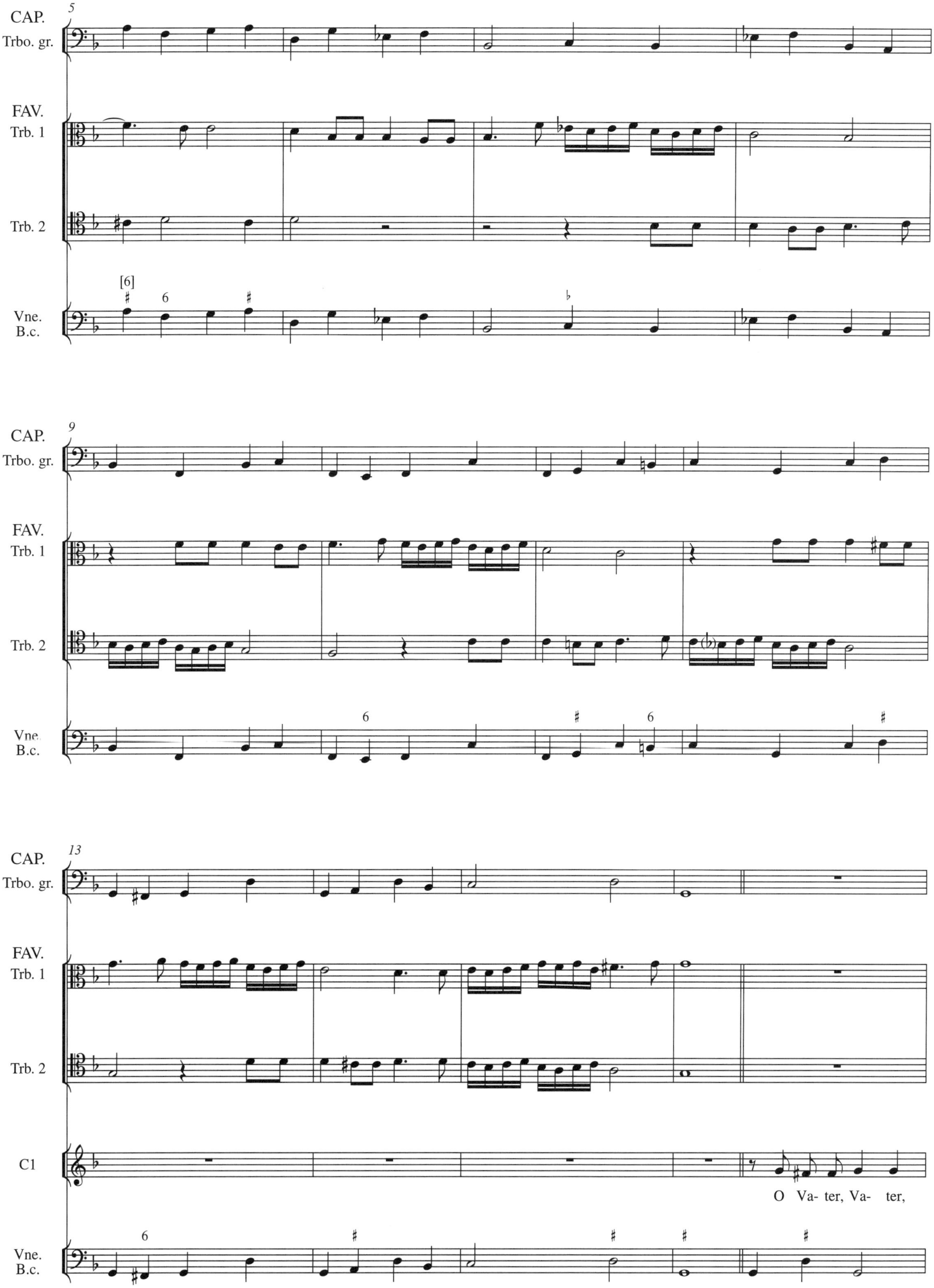
CAP.
Trbo. gr.
FAV.
Trb. 1
Trb. 2
Vne.
B.c.
C1
O Va- ter, Va- ter,

FAV.
C1
C2
Vne.
B.c.
B
al- ler Au- gen war- ten auff dich, o Va- ter, Va- ter, al- ler Au- gen war- ten auff dich,
O Va- ter, Va- ter,
(ɦ) al- ler Au- gen war- ten auff dich, ⟨al- ler Au- gen war- ten auff dich, al- ler Au- gen war- ten auff
o Va- ter, Va- ter, ⟨o Va- ter, Va- ter, o Va- ter,
Va- ter,⟩ al- ler Au- gen war- ten auff dich, o Va- ter, Va- ter, Va- ter, al- ler Au- gen war- ten auff
dich,⟩ o Va- ter, Va- ter, o Va- ter, Va- ter, Va- ter, al- ler Au- gen war- ten auff
dich.
dich.
Wer- det ihr mei- ne Ge- bo- the hal- ten, so wil ich euch Re- gen, Re- gen ge- ben zu

33
FAV.
C1
O Va- ter, Va- ter, al- ler Au- gen war- ten auff dich.
C2
O Va- ter, Va- ter, al- ler Au- gen war- ten auff dich.
B
sei- ner Zeit, wer- det ihr mei- ne Ge- bo- the
Vne.
B.c.
[6]
36
FAV.
C1
⟨Al- ler Au- gen war- ten auff dich.⟩
C2
⟨Al- ler Au- gen war- ten auff dich.⟩
B
hal- ten, so wil ich euch Re- gen, Re- gen ge- ben, das Land soll sein Ge- wäch- se
Vne.
B.c.
4
40
FAV.
C1
O Va- ter, Va- ter, ⟨o Va- ter, Va- ter,⟩ al- ler Au- gen war- ten auff
C2
O Va- ter, Va- ter, ⟨o Va- ter, Va- ter,⟩ al- ler Au- gen war- ten auff
B
ge- ben, das Land soll sein Ge- wäch- se ge- ben,
Vne.
B.c.
6

44
FAV.
C1
dich. O Va- ter, Va- ter, al- ler Au- gen war- ten auff
C2
dich. O Va- ter, Va- ter, al- ler Au- gen war- ten auff
B
die Bäu-me auff dem Fel-de sol-len ih-re Früch-te brin- gen,
Vne.
B.c.
48
FAV.
C1
dich. O Va- ter, Va- ter,
C2
dich. O Va- ter, Va- ter,
B
ihr sol- let Brods die Fül- le, Brods die Fül- le, die Fül- le, die Fül- le ha- ben,
Vne.
B.c.
51
FAV.
C1
al- ler Au- gen war- ten auff dich.
C2
al- ler Au- gen war- ten auff dich.
B
ihr sol- let Brods die Fül- le, die Fül- le, die Fül- le ha-
Vne.
B.c.

-ben.

O— Va- ter, du thust dei- ne mil- de Hand

O— Va- ter, du thust dei- ne mil- de Hand—

63
CAP.
Trbo. gr.
FAV.
Trb. 1
Trb. 2
C1
auff, o Va- ter, du thust dei- ne mil- de Hand auff,
C2
auff, o Va- ter, du thust dei- ne mil- de Hand auff,
Vne.
B.c.
67
CAP.
Trbo. gr.
FAV.
Trb. 1
Trb. 2
C1
du sät- ti- gest al- les, du sät- ti- gest al- les, al- les, was da le- bet,
C2
du sät- ti- gest al- les, du sät- ti- gest al- les, al- les, was da le- bet,
Vne.
B.c.

71
CAP.
Trbo. gr.
FAV.
Trb. 1
Trb. 2
C1
du sät- ti- gest al- les, du sät- ti- gest al- les,
C2
du sät- ti- gest al- les, du sät- ti- gest al- les,
Vne.
B.c.
74
CAP.
Trbo. gr.
FAV.
Trb. 1
Trb. 2
C1
al- les, was da le- bet. Al- ler Au- gen war- ten auff dich.
C2
al- les, was da le- bet. Al- ler Au- gen war- ten auff dich.
B
Wer- det ihr mei- ne Ge- bo- the hal- ten,
Vne.
B.c.

82

85
CAP.
Trbo. gr.
FAV.
Trb. 1
Trb. 2
C1
⟨Al- ler Au- gen war- ten auff dich.⟩ O Va- ter, Va- ter,
C2
⟨Al- ler Au- gen war- ten auff dich.⟩ O Va- ter, Va- ter,
B
ge- ben zu sei- ner Zeit, das Land soll sein Ge- wäch- se ge- ben, das
Vne.
B.c.
89
FAV.
C1
⟨o Va- ter, Va- ter,⟩ al- ler Au- gen war- ten auff dich.
C2
⟨o Va- ter, Va- ter,⟩ al- ler Au- gen war- ten auff dich.
B
Land soll sein Ge- wäch- se ge- ben, die Bäu- me auff dem
Vne.
B.c.

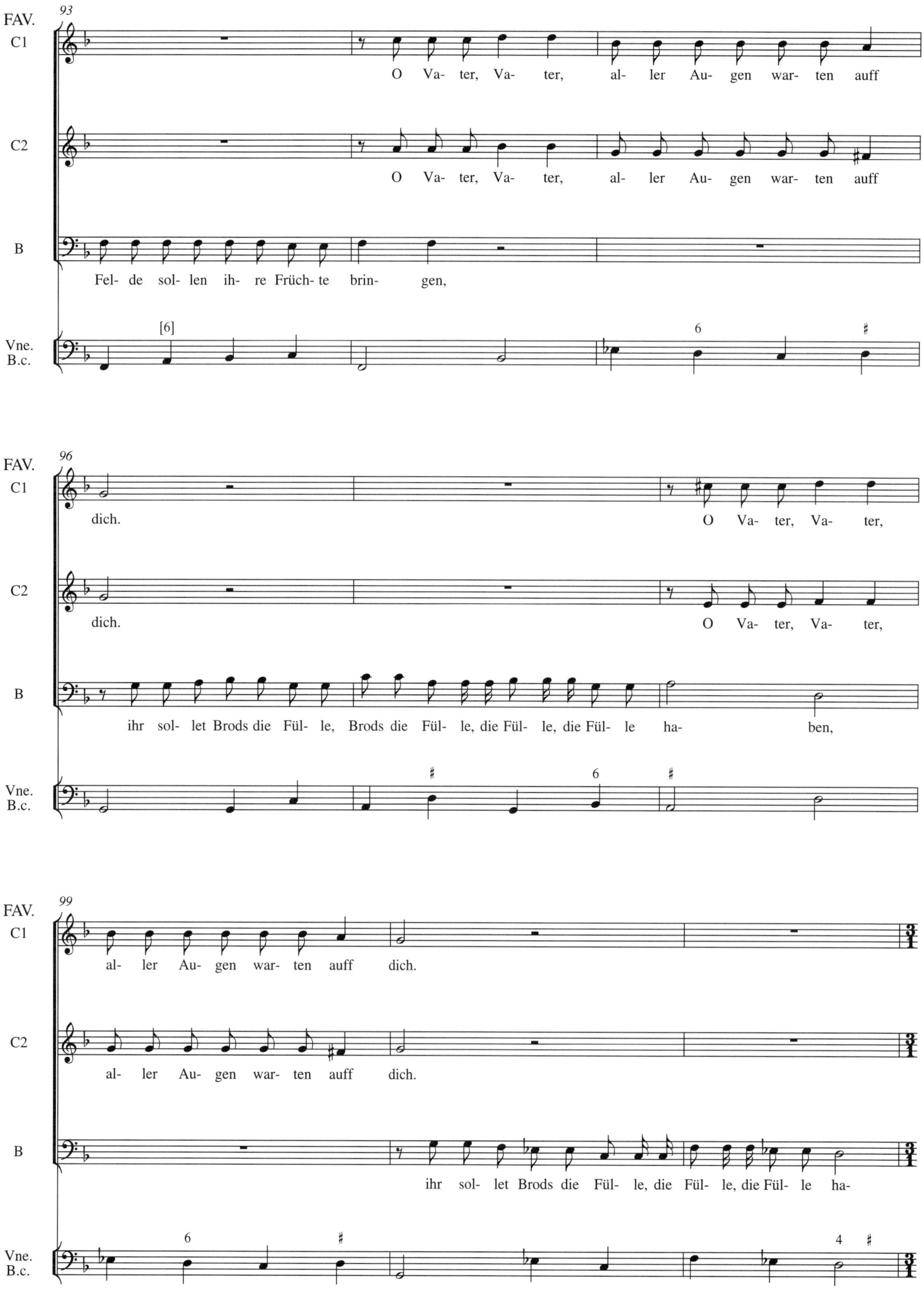

102
CAP.
C1
Ct. 1
Dan- cket dem Her- ren; denn er ist freund- lich,
C2
Ct. 2
Dan- cket dem Her- ren; denn er ist freund- lich,
A1
Trb. 1
Dan- cket dem Her- ren; denn er ist freund- lich,
A2
Trb. 2
Dan- cket dem Her- ren; denn er ist freund- lich,
T
Trb. 3
Dan- cket dem Her- ren; denn er ist freund- lich,
Trbo. gr.
B
Trbo. gr.
Dan- cket dem Her- ren; denn er ist freund- lich,
FAV.
Trb. 1
Trb. 2
C1
Dan- cket dem Her- ren; denn er ist freund- lich,
C2
Dan- cket dem Her- ren; denn er ist freund- lich,
B
-ben. Dan- cket dem Her- ren,
Vne.
B.c.

108
CAP.
C1 Ct. 1
denn er ist freund- lich,
C2 Ct. 2
⟨denn er ist freund- lich,⟩
A1 Trb. 1
denn er ist freund- lich,
A2 Trb. 2
⟨denn er ist freund- lich,⟩
T Trb. 3
⟨denn er ist freund- lich,⟩
B Trbo. gr.
Trbo. gr.
denn er ist freund- lich,
FAV.
Trb. 1
Trb. 2
C1
denn er ist freund- lich, sei- ne Gü- te wäh-ret e- wig-lich,
C2
denn er ist freund- lich, sei- ne Gü- te wäh-ret e- wig-lich,
B
⟨dan- cket dem Her- ren;⟩ denn er ist freund- lich, dan- cket dem Her- ren,
Vne. B.c.

114
CAP.
C1
Ct. 1
denn er ist
C2
Ct. 2
denn er ist
A1
Trb. 1
denn er ist
A2
Trb. 2
denn er ist
T
Trb. 3
denn er ist
B
Trbo. gr.
denn er ist
FAV.
Trb. 1
Trb. 2
C1
⟨sei- ne Gü- te wäh- ret e- wig- lich, sei- ne Gü- te wäh- ret e- wig- lich,⟩ denn er ist
C2
⟨sei- ne Gü- te wäh- ret e- wig- lich, sei- ne Gü- te wäh- ret e- wig- lich,⟩ denn er ist
B
⟨dan- cket dem Her- ren, dan- cket dem Her- ren;⟩ denn er ist
Vne.
B.c.

119
CAP.
C1 Ct. 1
freund- lich, dan- cket dem Her- ren,
C2 Ct. 2
freund- lich, dan- cket dem Her- ren,
A1 Trb. 1
freund- lich, dan- cket dem Her- ren,
A2 Trb. 2
freund- lich, dan- cket dem Her- ren,
T Trb. 3
freund- lich, dan- cket dem Her- ren,
B Trbo. gr.
freund- lich, dan- cket dem_ Her- ren,
FAV.
Trb. 1
Trb. 2
C1
freund- lich, dan- cket dem Her- ren, ⟨dan- cket dem Her- ren,
C2
freund- lich, dan- cket dem Her- ren, ⟨dan- cket dem Her- ren,
B
freund- lich, sei- ne Gü- te wäh- ret e- wig- lich, ⟨sei- ne Gü- te wäh- ret e- wig- lich,
Vne. B.c.

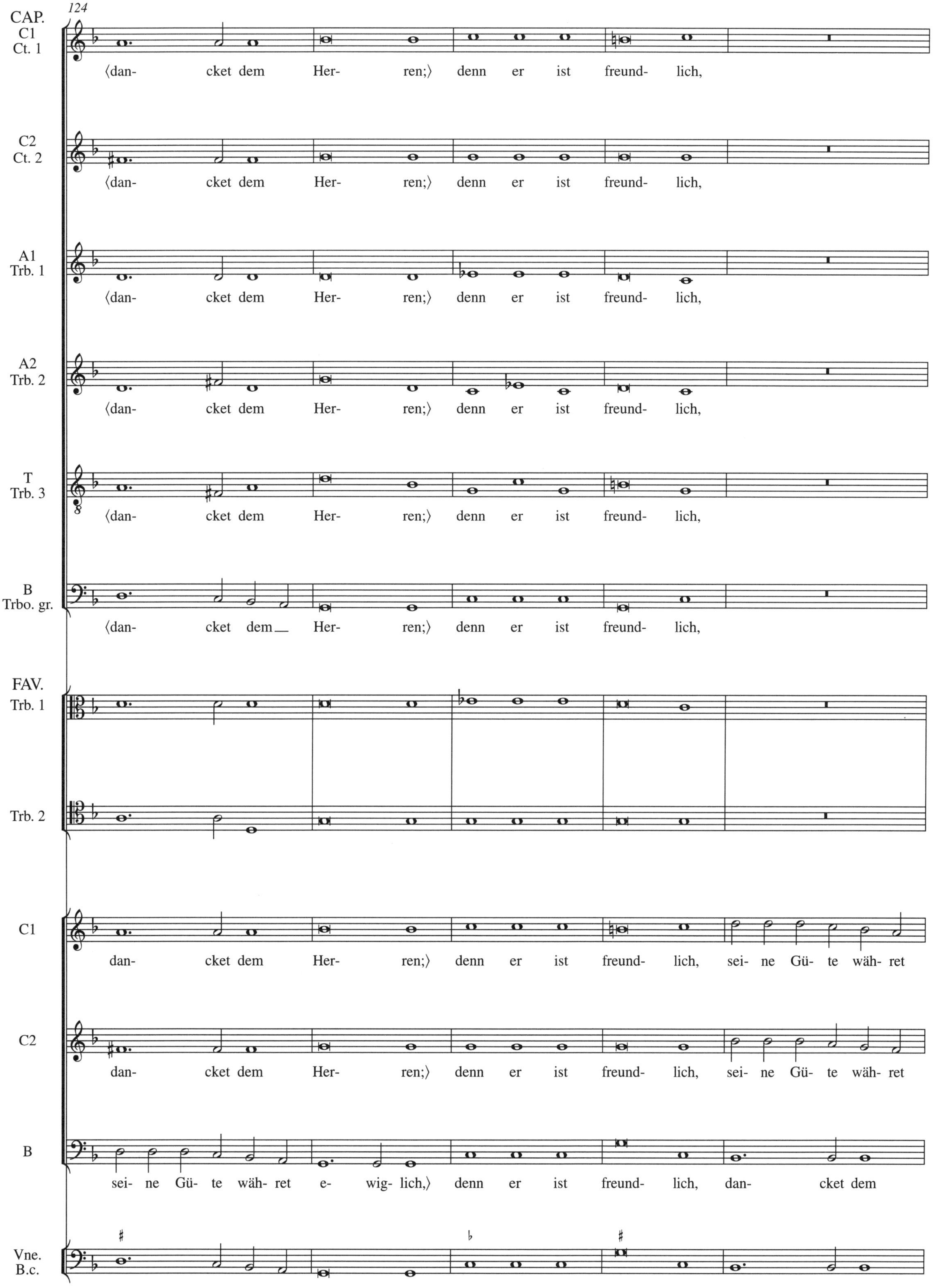

129
CAP.
C1 Ct. 1
sei- ne Gü- te wäh-ret e- wig- lich, sei- ne Gü- te wäh- ret e- wig- lich.
C2 Ct. 2
sei- ne Gü- te wäh- ret e- wig- lich, sei- ne Gü- te wäh- ret e- wig- lich.
A1 Trb. 1
sei- ne Gü- te wäh-ret e- wig- lich, sei- ne Gü- te wäh- ret e- wig- lich.
A2 Trb. 2
⟨sei- ne Gü- te wäh-ret e- wig- lich, sei- ne Gü- te wäh- ret e- wig- lich.
T Trb. 3
sei- ne Gü- te wäh-ret e- wig- lich, sei- ne Gü- te wäh- ret e- wig- lich.
B Trbo. gr.
sei- ne Gü- te wäh-ret e- wig- lich, ⟨sei- ne Gü- te wäh- ret e- wig- lich.⟩
FAV.
Trb. 1
Trb. 2
C1
e- wig- lich, ⟨sei- ne Gü- te wäh-ret e- wig- lich, sei- ne Gü- te wäh- ret e- wig- lich.⟩
C2
e- wig- lich, ⟨sei- ne Gü- te wäh-ret e- wig- lich, sei- ne Gü- te wäh- ret e- wig- lich.⟩
B
Her- ren, ⟨dan- cket dem Her- ren, dan- cket dem Her- ren,⟩
Vne. B.c.

134
CAP.
C1
Ct. 1
Dan- cket, dan- cket, dan- cket dem Her- ren; sei- - ne Gü- te
C2
Ct. 2
Dan- cket, dan- cket, dan- cket dem Her- ren; sei- - ne Gü- te
A1
Trb. 1
Dan- cket, dan- cket, dan- cket dem Her- ren; sei- - ne Gü- te
A2
Trb. 2
Dan- cket, dan- cket, dan- cket dem Her- ren; sei- - ne Gü- te
T
Trb. 3
Dan- cket, dan- cket, dan- cket dem Her- ren; sei- - ne Gü- te
B
Trbo. gr.
Dan- cket, dan- cket, dan- cket dem Her- ren; sei- - ne Gü- te
FAV.
Trb. 1
Trb. 2
C1
Dan- cket, dan- cket, dan- cket dem Her- ren; sei- - ne Gü- te
C2
Dan- cket, dan- cket, dan- cket dem Her- ren; sei- - ne Gü- te
B
dan- cket, dan- cket, dan- cket dem Her- ren; sei- - ne Gü- te
Vne.
B.c.
6

140
CAP.
C1
Ct. 1
wäh- ret e- wig- lich, e- - wig- lich.
C2
Ct. 2
wäh- - ret e- - wig- lich.
A1
Trb. 1
wäh- ret e- - wig- lich, e- wig- lich.
A2
Trb. 2
wäh- ret e- wig- lich, e- - wig- lich.
T
Trb. 3
wäh- ret e- wig- lich, e- wig- lich, e- wig- lich.
B
Trbo. gr.
wäh- ret e- wig- lich, e- - wig- lich.
FAV.
Trb. 1
Trb. 2
C1
wäh- ret e- - - wig- lich.
C2
wäh- - ret e- - wig- lich.
B
wäh- ret e- - wig- lich.
Vne.
B.c.

Gott fähret auff mit Jauchtzen!

FAV.
C1
Gott fäh- ret auff, ⟨Gott fäh- ret auff, Gott fäh- ret auff⟩ mit Jauch-tzen, ⟨mit Jauch- tzen!⟩
A
Trb. 1
Fro- lo- cket mit
T
Trb. 2
Fro- lo- cket mit
[6]
Vne.
B.c.
CAP.
C
Ct.
al- le, al- le, al- le Völ- cker.
A
Trb. 1
al- le, al- le, al- le Völ- cker.
T
Trb. 2
al- le, al- le, ⟨al- le⟩ Völ- cker.
B
Trbo. gr.
al- le, al- le, al- le Völ- cker.
FAV.
Clno. 1 or
Tbta. 1
Clno. 2 or
Tbta. 2
C1
al- le, al- le, al- le Völ- cker.
C2
al- le, al- le, al- le Völ- cker.
A
Trb. 1
Hän- den, ⟨fro- lo- cket mit Hän- den,⟩ al- le, al- le, al- le Völ- cker.
T
Trb. 2
Hän- den, ⟨fro- lo- cket mit Hän- den,⟩ al- le, al- le, al- le Völ- cker.
B
Fro- lo- cket mit Hän- den, al- le, al- le, al- le Völ- cker. Gott fäh- ret
6
Vne.
B.c.

17
FAV.
C1
Gott fäh- ret auff, ⟨Gott fäh- ret auff, Gott fäh- ret auff⟩ mit
C2
Gott fäh- ret auff, ⟨Gott fäh- ret auff, Gott fäh- ret auff⟩ mit
B
auff, ⟨Gott fäh-ret auff, Gott fäh- ret auff,
Gott fäh- ret
Vne.
B.c.
20
CAP.
C
Ct.
al- le, al- le,
A
Trb. 1
al- le, al- le,
T
Trb. 2
al- le, ⟨al- le,⟩
B
Trbo. gr.
al- le, al- le,
FAV.
Clno. 1 or
Tbta. 1
Clno. 2 or
Tbta. 2
C1
Jauch- tzen, ⟨mit Jauch- tzen!⟩
al- le, al- le,
C2
Jauch- tzen, ⟨mit Jauch- tzen!⟩
al- le, al- le,
A
Trb. 1
Fro- lo- cket mit Hän- den, al- le, al- le,
T
Trb. 2
Fro- lo- cket mit Hän- den, al- le, al- le,
B
auff⟩ mit Jauch- tzen!
Fro- lo- cket mit Hän- den, al- le, al- le,
[4 3]
Vne.
B.c.

24
CAP.
C
Ct.
al- le Völ- cker. Fro- lo- cket mit Hän- den und jauch- tzet, fro- lo- cket und jauch-tzet Gott mit
A
Trb. 1
al- le Völ- cker. Fro- lo- cket mit Hän- den und jauch- tzet, fro- lo- cket und jauch-tzet Gott mit
T
Trb. 2
al- le Völ- cker. Fro- lo- cket mit Hän- den und jauch- tzet, fro- lo- cket und jauch-tzet Gott mit
B
Trbo. gr.
al- le Völ- cker. Fro- lo- cket mit Hän- den und jauch- tzet, fro- lo- cket und jauch-tzet Gott mit
FAV.
Clno. 1 or
Tbta. 1
Clno. 2 or
Tbta. 2
C1
al- le Völ- cker. Fro- lo- cket mit Hän- den und jauch- tzet, fro- lo- cket und jauch-tzet Gott mit
C2
al- le Völ- cker. Fro- lo- cket mit Hän- den und jauch- tzet, fro- lo- cket und jauch-tzet Gott mit
A
Trb. 1
al- le Völ- cker. Fro- lo- cket mit Hän- den und jauch- tzet, fro- lo- cket und jauch-tzet Gott mit
T
Trb. 2
al- le Völ- cker. Fro- lo- cket mit Hän- den und jauch- tzet, fro- lo- cket und jauch-tzet Gott mit
B
al- le Völ- cker. Fro- lo- cket mit Hän- den und jauch- tzet, fro- lo- cket und jauch-tzet Gott mit
6
Vne.
B.c.

28
CAP.
C
Ct.
frö- li- chen Schal- le!
A
Trb. 1
frö- li- chen Schal- le!
T
Trb. 2
frö- li- chen Schal- le!
B
Trbo. gr.
frö- li- chen Schal- le!
FAV.
Clno. 1 or
Tbta. 1
Clno. 2 or
Tbta. 2
C1
frö- li- chen Schal- le! Denn der Herr, der Al- ler- höch- ste, ist er- schreck-
C2
frö- li- chen Schal- le! Denn der Herr, der Al- ler- höch- ste, ist er- schreck-
A
Trb. 1
frö- li- chen Schal- le!
T
Trb. 2
frö- li- chen Schal- le!
B
frö- li- chen Schal- le!
Vne.
B.c.

32
FAV.
C1
-lich, ⟨denn der Herr, der Al- ler- höch-ste, ist er-schreck-
C2
-lich, denn der Herr, der Al- ler- höch-ste, ist er- schreck-
A
Trb. 1
Denn der Herr, der Al- ler- höch-ste, ist er-schreck- lich,
T
Trb. 2
Denn der Herr, der Al- ler- höch-ste, ist er- schreck- lich,
Vne.
B.c.
36
CAP.
C
Ct.
Denn der Herr, der Al- ler- höch- ste, ist er-schreck-
A
Trb. 1
Denn der Herr, der Al- ler- höch- ste, ist er-schreck-
T
Trb. 2
Denn der Herr, der Al- ler- höch- ste, ist er-schreck-
B
Trbo. gr.
Denn der Herr, der Al- ler- höch- ste, ist er-schreck-
FAV.
Clno. 1 or
Tbta. 1
Clno. 2 or
Tbta. 2
C1
-lich, denn der Herr, der Al- ler- höch- ste, ist er-schreck-
C2
-lich, ⟨denn der Herr, der Al- ler- höch- ste, ist er- schreck-
A
Trb. 1
⟨denn der Herr, der Al- ler- höch-ste, ist er- schreck- lich, ⟨denn der Herr, der Al- ler- höch- ste, ist er-schreck-
T
Trb. 2
denn der Herr, der Al- ler- höch-ste, ist er- schreck- lich, ⟨denn der Herr, der Al- ler- höch- ste, ist er-schreck-
B
Denn der Herr, der Al- ler- höch- ste, ist er-schreck-
Vne.
B.c.

40
CAP.
C
Ct.
-lich, ein gros- ser, gros- ser Kö- nig auff den gan- tzen Erd- bo- den.
A
Trb. 1
-lich, ein gros- ser, gros- ser Kö- nig auff den gan- tzen Erd- bo- den.
T
Trb. 2
-lich, ein gros- ser, gros- ser Kö- nig auff den gan- tzen Erd- bo- den.
B
Trbo. gr.
-lich, ein gros- ser, gros- ser Kö- nig auff den gan- tzen Erd- bo- den.
FAV.
Clno. 1 or
Tbta. 1
Clno. 2 or
Tbta. 2
C1
-lich,〉 ein gros- ser, gros- ser Kö- nig auff den gan- tzen Erd- bo- den.
C2
-lich,〉 ein gros- ser, gros- ser Kö- nig auff den gan- tzen Erd- bo- den.
A
Trb. 1
-lich,〉 ein gros- ser, gros- ser Kö- nig auff den gan- tzen Erd- bo- den.
T
Trb. 2
-lich,〉 ein gros- ser, gros- ser Kö- nig auff den gan- tzen Erd- bo- den.
B
-lich, ein gros- ser, gros- ser Kö- nig auff den gan- tzen Erd- bo- den.
Vne.
B.c.
4 ♯

44
CAP.
Trb. 2
Trbo. gr.
FAV.
Clno. 1 or Tbta. 1
Clno. 2 or Tbta. 2
Trb. 1
Trb. 2
B
Er wird die Völ-cker, die Völ-cker un- ter uns, un- ter uns zwin- gen,
Vne. B.c.
[4] ♯

47
CAP.
Trb. 2
Trbo. gr.
FAV.
Trb. 1
Trb. 2
B
er wird die Völ-cker, die Völ-cker, die Völ-cker, die Völ-cker un- ter uns, un- ter uns zwin-
Vne. B.c.
4 ♯ ♭

101

-gen ... und die Leu- te un- ter un- sre Füs- se. Er wird die Völ- cker, die Völ- cker, ⟨die Völ- cker, die Völ- cker⟩

Er wird die Völ- cker, die Völ- cker, die Völ- cker, die Völ- cker

Er wird die Völ- cker, die Völ- cker, ⟨die Völ- cker, die Völ- cker⟩

Er wird die Völ- cker, ⟨die Völ- cker,⟩ die Völ- cker, ⟨die Völ- cker⟩

Er wird die Völ- cker, die Völ- cker, ⟨die Völ- cker, die Völ- cker⟩

Er wird die Völ- cker, die Völ- cker, die Völ- cker, die Völ- cker

Er wird die Völ- cker, die Völ- cker, ⟨die Völ- cker, die Völ- cker⟩

Er wird die Völ- cker, die Völ- cker, die Völ- cker, die Völ- cker

56
CAP.
C
Ct.
un- ter uns, ⟨un- ter uns⟩ zwin- gen und die Leu- te un- ter un- sre Füs- se.
A
Trb. 1
un- ter uns, un- ter uns zwin- gen und die Leu- te un- ter un- sre Füs- se.
T
Trb. 2
un- ter uns, ⟨un- ter uns⟩ zwin- gen und die Leu- te un- ter un- sre Füs- se.
B
Trbo. gr.
un- ter uns, ⟨un- ter uns⟩ zwin-gen und die Leu- te un- ter un- sre Füs- se.
FAV.
Clno. 1 or
Tbta. 1
Clno. 2 or
Tbta. 2
C1
un- ter uns, ⟨un- ter uns⟩ zwin- gen und die Leu- te un- ter un- sre Füs- se.
C2
un- ter uns, un- ter uns zwin- gen und die Leu- te un- ter un- sre Füs- se.
A
Trb. 1
un- ter uns, un- ter uns zwin- gen und die Leu- te un- ter un- sre Füs- se.
T
Trb. 2
un- ter uns, un- ter uns zwin- gen und die Leu- te un- ter un- sre Füs- se.
B
un- ter uns, un- ter uns zwin-gen und die Leu- te un- ter un- sre Füs- se.
Vne.
B.c.
[♯]
[4 3]
6

60
CAP.
C
Ct.
Er er-weh- let uns zum Erb- theil, ⟨er er-weh-let uns zum Erb- theil,⟩ zum
A
Trb. 1
Er er-weh- let uns, ⟨er er-weh- let uns,⟩ uns, er er-weh-let uns, er er-weh- let uns zum
T
Trb. 2
Er er-weh- let uns zum Erb- theil, ⟨er er-weh-let uns zum Erb- theil,⟩ zum
B
Trbo. gr.
Er er-weh- let uns zum Erb- theil, ⟨er er-weh- let uns zum
FAV.
Clno. 1 or
Tbta. 1
Clno. 2 or
Tbta. 2
C1
Er er-weh- let uns zum Erb- theil, ⟨er er-weh-let uns zum Erb- theil,⟩ zum
C2
Er er-weh- let uns, ⟨er er-weh- let uns⟩ zum Erb- theil, er er-weh- let uns zum
A
Trb. 1
Er er-weh- let uns, er er-weh- let uns, uns, er er-weh-let uns, er er-weh- let uns zum
T
Trb. 2
Er er-weh- let uns zum Erb- theil, ⟨er er-weh-let uns zum Erb- theil,⟩ zum
B
Er er-weh- let uns zum Erb- theil, ⟨er er-weh- let uns zum
Vne.
B.c.

64
CAP.
C
Ct.
Erb- theil, die Herr- lig- keit Ja- cob, den er lie- bet. Se- la, Se- la.
A
Trb. 1
Erb- theil, die Herr- lig- keit Ja- cob, den er lie- bet. Se- la, Se- la.
T
Trb. 2
Erb- theil, die Herr- lig- keit Ja- cob, den er lie- bet. Se- la, Se- la.
B
Trbo. gr.
Erb- theil,〉 die Herr- lig- keit Ja- cob, den er lie- bet. Se- la, Se- la.
FAV.
Clno. 1 or
Tbta. 1
Clno. 2 or
Tbta. 2
C1
Erb- theil, die Herr- lig- keit Ja- cob, den er lie- bet. Se- la, Se- la.
C2
Erb- theil, die Herr- lig- keit Ja- cob, den er lie- bet. Se- la, Se- la.
A
Trb. 1
Erb- theil, die Herr- lig- keit Ja- cob, den er lie- bet. Se- la, Se- la.
T
Trb. 2
Erb- theil, die Herr- lig- keit Ja- cob, den er lie- bet. Se- la, Se- la.
B
Erb- theil,〉 die Herr- lig- keit Ja- cob, den er lie- bet. Se- la, Se- la.
Vne.
B.c.
[4 3]

Gott fäh- ret auff, ⟨Gott fäh- ret

78
FAV.
C1
Gott fäh- ret auff, ⟨Gott fähr- et auff, Gott fäh- ret auff, Gott fähr- et auff⟩ mit
C2
Gott fäh- ret auff, ⟨Gott fäh- ret auff, Gott fäh- ret auff, Gott fäh- ret auff⟩ mit
B
auff, Gott fäh- ret auff, Gott fäh- ret auff, Gott fäh- ret
Vne.
B.c.
81
CAP.
C
Ct.
und der Herr, der Herr, ⟨der Herr⟩ mit hel- ler Po- sau-
A
Trb. 1
und der Herr, der Herr, ⟨der Herr⟩ mit hel- ler Po- sau-
T
Trb. 2
und der Herr, der Herr, ⟨der Herr⟩ mit hel- ler Po- sau-
B
Trbo. gr.
und der Herr, der Herr, der Herr mit hel- ler Po- sau-
FAV.
C1
Jauch- tzen und der Herr, der Herr, ⟨der Herr⟩ mit hel- ler Po- sau-
C2
Jauch- tzen und der Herr, der Herr, der Herr mit hel- ler Po- sau-
A
Trb. 1
und der Herr, der Herr, der Herr mit hel- ler Po- sau-
T
Trb. 2
und der Herr, der Herr, der Herr mit hel- ler Po- sau-
B
auff⟩ mit Jauch- tzen und der Herr, der Herr, der Herr mit hel- ler Po- sau-
Vne.
B.c.

85
CAP.
C
Ct.
-nen. Lob- sin- get Gott, ⟨lob- sin- get Gott,⟩ lob- sin- get, sin- get Gott, lob- sin- get Gott, lob-
A
Trb. 1
-nen. Lob- sin- get Gott, lob- sin- get Gott, lob- sin- get, sin- get Gott, lob- sin- get, sin- get
T
Trb. 2
-nen. Lob- sin- get, sin- get Gott, ⟨lob- sin- get, sin- get Gott,⟩ lob- sin- get, sin- get
B
Trbo. gr.
-nen. Lob- sin- get, sin- get Gott,
FAV.
Clno. 1 or
Tbta. 1
Clno. 2 or
Tbta. 2
C1
-nen. Lob- sin- get Gott, lob- sin- get Gott, lob- sin- get, sin- get Gott, lob- sin- get Gott, lob-
C2
-nen. Lob- sin- get Gott, ⟨lob- sin- get Gott,⟩ lob- sin- get, sin- get
A
Trb. 1
-nen. Lob- sin- get Gott, lob- sin- get Gott, lob- sin- get, sin- get Gott, lob- sin- get, sin- get
T
Trb. 2
-nen. Lob- sin- get, sin- get Gott, ⟨lob- sin- get, sin- get Gott, lob- sin- get, sin- get
B
-nen. Lob- sin- get, sin- get Gott,
Vne.
B.c.
6

88
CAP.
C
Ct.
-sin- get Gott, lob- sin- get, sin- get Gott, lob- sin- get un- - serm Kö- ni-
A
Trb. 1
Gott, lob- sin- get, sin- get Gott, lob- sin- get un- serm Kö- ni-
T
Trb. 2
Gott, ⟨lob- sin- get, sin- get Gott,⟩ lob- sin- get un- serm, un- serm Kö- ni-
B
Trbo. gr.
lob- sin- get, sin- get Gott, lob- sin- get un- serm Kö- ni-
FAV.
Clno. 1 or
Tbta. 1
Clno. 2 or
Tbta. 2
C1
-sin- get Gott, lob- sin- get, sin- get Gott, lob- sin- get un- - serm Kö- ni-
C2
Gott, lob- sin- get Gott, lob- sin- get, sin- get un- serm Kö- ni-
A
Trb. 1
Gott, lob- sin- get, sin- get Gott, lob- sin- get un- serm Kö- ni-
T
Trb. 2
Gott, lob- sin- get, sin- get Gott,⟩ lob- sin- get un- serm, un- serm Kö- ni-
B
⟨lob- sin- get, sin- get Gott,⟩ lob- sin- get un- serm Kö- ni-
Vne.
B.c.
[7 6]
♯ 4 ♯

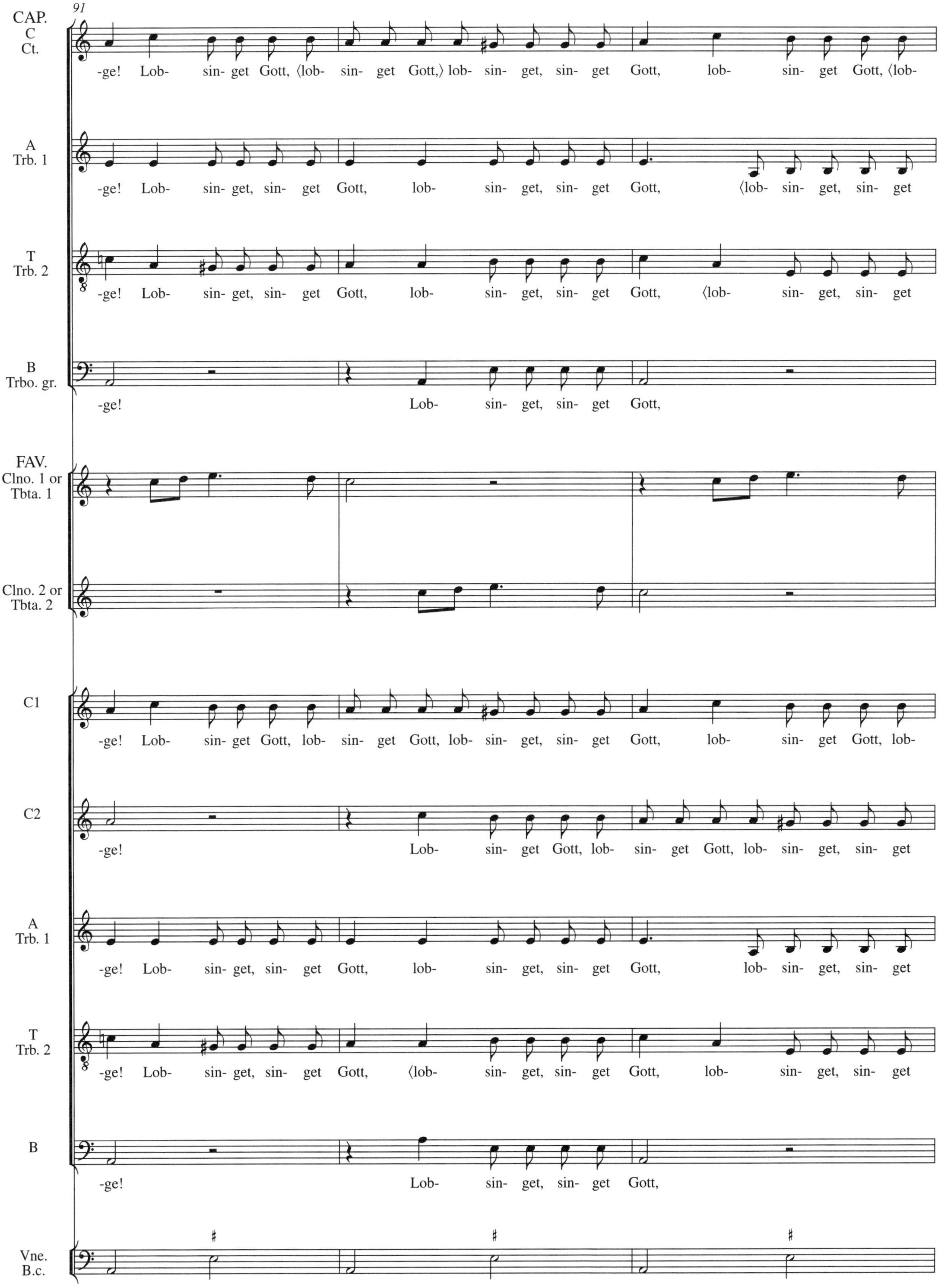

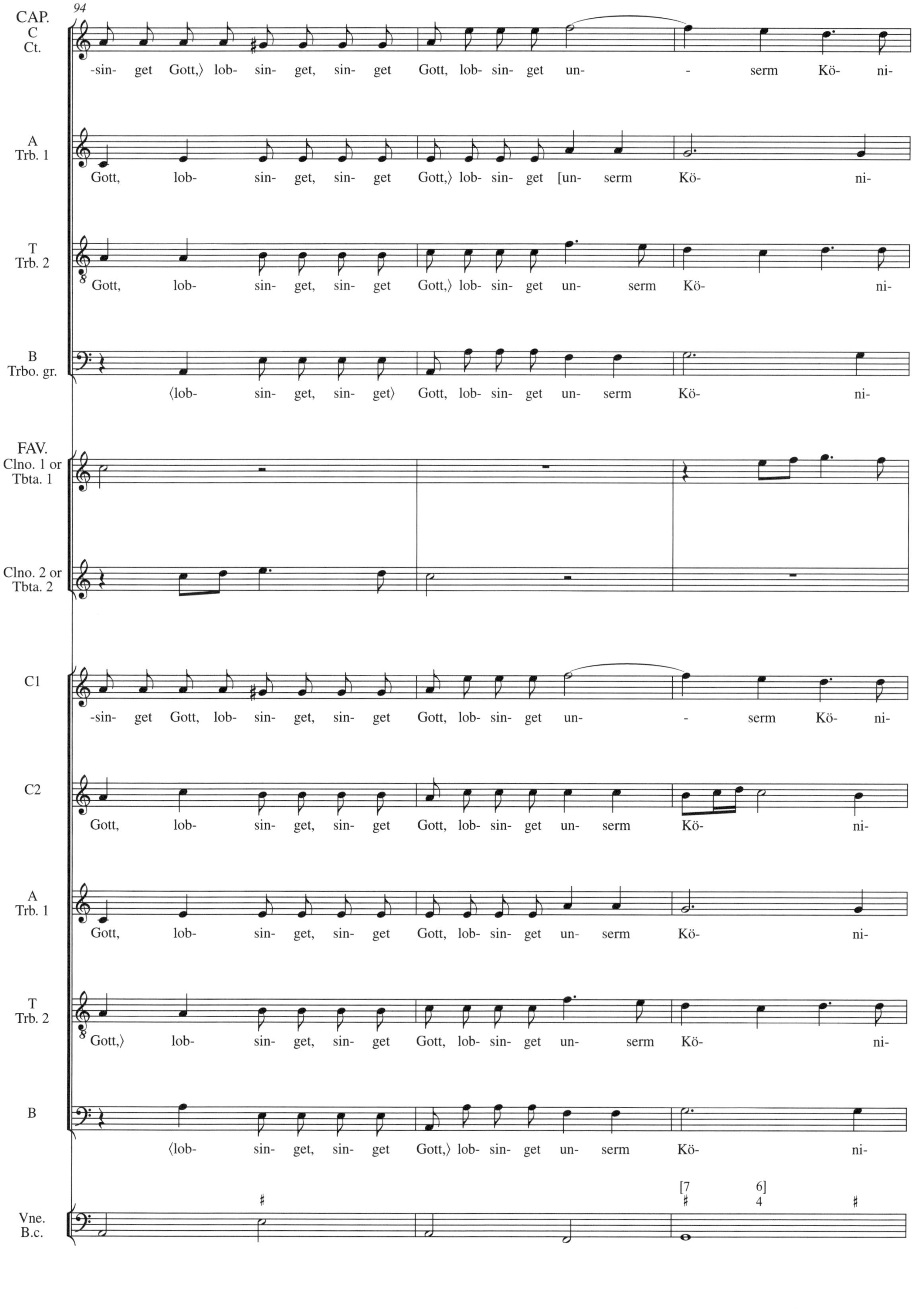

97
CAP.
C
Ct.
-ge! Lob- sin- get Gott, ⟨lob- sin- get Gott,⟩ lob- sin- get, sin- get Gott, lob- sin- get, sin- get
A
Trb. 1
-ge! Lob- sin- get, sin- get Gott, lob- sin- get, sin- get Gott, lob- sin- get, sin- get
T
Trb. 2
-ge! Lob- sin- get, sin- get Gott, lob- sin- get, sin- get Gott, ⟨lob- sin- get, sin- get
B
Trbo. gr.
-ge! Lob- sin- get, sin- get Gott,
FAV.
Clno. 1 or
Tbta. 1
Clno. 2 or
Tbta. 2
C1
-ge! Lob- sin- get Gott, ⟨lob- sin- get Gott,⟩ lob- sin- get, sin- get Gott, lob- sin- get, sin- get
C2
-ge! Lob- sin- get Gott, ⟨lob- sin- get Gott,⟩ lob- sin- get, sin- get
A
Trb. 1
-ge! Lob- sin- get, sin- get Gott, lob- sin- get, sin- get Gott, lob- sin- get, sin- get
T
Trb. 2
-ge! Lob- sin- get, sin- get Gott, ⟨lob- sin- get, sin- get Gott, lob- sin- get, sin- get
B
-ge! Lob- sin- get, sin- get Gott,
Vne.
B.c.
6

100
CAP.
C
Ct.
Gott, lob-sin-get un- - serm Kö- ni- ge!
A
Trb. 1
Gott, lob-sin-get] un-serm Kö- ni- ge!
T
Trb. 2
Gott,⟩ lob-sin-get un-serm Kö- ni- ge!
B
Trbo. gr.
lob-sin-get un-serm Kö- ni- ge!
FAV.
Clno. 1 or
Tbta. 1
Clno. 2 or
Tbta. 2
C1
Gott, lob-sin-get un- - serm Kö- ni- ge!
C2
Gott, lob-sin-get un-serm Kö- ni- ge!
A
Trb. 1
Gott, lob-sin-get un-serm Kö- ni- ge!
T
Trb. 2
Gott,⟩ lob-sin-get un-serm Kö- ni- ge!
B
lob-sin-get un-serm Kö- ni- ge!
[7 6]
Vne.
B.c.

105
CAP.
C
Ct.
A
Trb. 1
T
Trb. 2
B
Trbo. gr.
FAV.
Clno. 1 or
Tbta. 1
Clno. 2 or
Tbta. 2
C1
Al- le- lu- ja, al- le- lu- ja, ⟨al- le- lu- ja, al- le- lu- ja!⟩
C2
Al- le- lu- ja, ⟨al- le- lu- ja,⟩ al- le- lu- ja, ⟨al- le- lu- ja!⟩
A
Trb. 1
Al- le- lu- ja, ⟨al- le-
T
Trb. 2
Al- le- lu- ja, ⟨al- le-
B
Al- le- lu- ja, al- le- lu- ja, al- le- lu- ja, al- le- lu- ja! Al- le- lu- ja, ⟨al- le-
Vne.
B.c.
[6]
[4]

110
CAP.
C
Ct.
A
Trb. 1
Al- le- lu- ja, al- le-
T
Trb. 2
Al- le- lu- ja, ⟨al- le-
B
Trbo. gr.
FAV.
Clno. 1 or
Tbta. 1
Clno. 2 or
Tbta. 2
C1
Al- le- lu- ja, al- le- lu- ja,
C2
Al- le- lu- ja, ⟨al- le- lu- ja,⟩
A
Trb. 1
-lu- ja, al- le- lu- ja, al- le- lu- ja! Al- le- lu- ja, al- le-
T
Trb. 2
-lu- ja, al- le- lu- ja,⟩ al- le- lu- ja! Al- le- lu- ja, ⟨al- le-
B
-lu- ja, al- le- lu- ja, al- le- lu- ja! Al- le- lu- ja, al- le- lu- ja,
[6] [4 3]
Vne.
B.c.

115
CAP.
C
Ct.
Al- le- lu- ja, ⟨al- le- lu- ja, al- le- lu- ja!⟩
A
Trb. 1
-lu- ja, al- le- lu- ja, ⟨al- le- lu- ja,⟩ al- le- lu- ja!
T
Trb. 2
-lu- ja,⟩ al- le- lu- ja, ⟨al- le- lu- ja, al- le- lu- ja!⟩
B
Trbo. gr.
Al- le- lu- ja, al- le- lu- ja, ⟨al- le- lu- ja!⟩
FAV.
Clno. 1 or
Tbta. 1
Clno. 2 or
Tbta. 2
C1
⟨al- le- lu- ja, al- le- lu- ja,⟩ al- le- lu- ja! ⟨Al- le- lu- ja, al- le-
C2
al- le- lu- ja, ⟨al- le- lu- ja, al- le- lu- ja!⟩ Al- le- lu- ja, ⟨al- le-
A
Trb. 1
-lu- ja,⟩ al- le- lu- ja, ⟨al- le- lu- ja, al- le- lu- ja!
T
Trb. 2
-lu- ja, al- le- lu- ja, al- le- lu- ja, al- le- lu- ja!⟩
B
al- le- lu- ja, al- le- lu- ja, al- le- lu- ja! Al- le- lu- ja, al- le-
Vne.
B.c.

120
CAP.
C
Ct.
Al- le- lu- ja, ⟨al- le- lu- ja, al- le- lu- ja!
A
Trb. 1
Al- le- lu- ja, ⟨al- le- lu- ja,⟩ al- le- lu- ja, ⟨al- le- lu- ja,⟩ al- le- lu- ja!
T
Trb. 2
Al- le- lu- ja, ⟨al- le- lu- ja, al- le- lu- ja, al- le- lu- ja,⟩ al- le- lu- ja!
B
Trbo. gr.
Al- le- lu- ja, ⟨al- le- lu- ja,⟩ al- le- lu- ja!
FAV.
Clno. 1 or
Tbta. 1
Clno. 2 or
Tbta. 2
C1
-lu- ja, al- le- lu- ja, al- le- lu- ja,⟩ al- le- lu- ja!
C2
-lu- ja,⟩ al- le- lu- ja, ⟨al- le- lu- ja, al- le- lu- ja!⟩
A
Trb. 1
Al- le- lu- ja, al- le- lu- ja, al- le- lu- ja,⟩ al- le- [lu- ja,] al- le- lu- ja!
T
Trb. 2
Al- le- lu- ja, ⟨al- le- lu- ja, al- le- lu- ja, al- le- lu- ja,⟩ al- le- lu- ja!
B
-lu- ja, al- le- lu- ja, al- le- lu- ja, al- le- lu- ja!
Vne.
B.c.

117

130
CAP.
C
Ct.
-ja! Al- le- lu- ja, al- le- lu- ja, al- le- lu- ja, al- le- lu- ja,〉
A
Trb. 1
-ja!〉 Al- le- lu- ja, 〈al- le- lu- ja, al- le- lu- ja, al- le- lu- ja,〉
T
Trb. 2
-ja!〉 Al- le- lu- ja, 〈al- le- lu- ja, al- le- lu- ja,〉 al- le- lu- ja,
B
Trbo. gr.
-ja!〉 Al- le- lu- ja, 〈al- le- lu- ja,〉 al- le- lu- ja, al- le- lu- ja,
FAV.
Clno. 1 or
Tbta. 1
Clno. 2 or
Tbta. 2
C1
-ja! 〈Al- le- lu- ja, al- le- lu- ja, al- le- lu- ja, al- le- lu- ja,〉
C2
-ja!〉 Al- le- lu- ja, 〈al- le- lu- ja,〉 al- le- lu- ja, 〈al- le- lu- ja,
A
Trb. 1
-ja!〉 Al- le- lu- ja, 〈al- le- lu- ja, al- le- lu- ja, al- le- lu- ja,〉
T
Trb. 2
-ja! 〈Al- le- lu- ja, al- le- lu- ja, al- le- lu- ja, al- le- lu- ja,〉
B
-ja! Al- le- lu- ja, al- le- lu- ja, al- le- lu- ja, al- le- lu- ja,
Vne.
B.c.

135
CAP.
C
Ct.
al- le- lu- ja! Al- le- lu- ja, ⟨al- le- lu- ja, al- le- lu- ja, al- le-
A
Trb. 1
al- le- lu- ja! Al- le- lu- ja, ⟨al- le- lu- ja, al- le- lu- ja, al- le-
T
Trb. 2
⟨al- le- lu- ja!⟩ Al- le- lu- ja, ⟨al- le- lu- ja, al- le- lu- ja, al- le-
B
Trbo. gr.
⟨al- le- lu- ja!⟩ Al- le- lu- ja, ⟨al- le- lu- ja,⟩ al- le- lu- ja, ⟨al- le-
FAV.
Clno. 1 or
Tbta. 1
Clno. 2 or
Tbta. 2
C1
al- le- lu- ja! ⟨Al- le- lu- ja, al- le- lu- ja, al- le- lu- ja, al- le-
C2
al- le- lu- ja!⟩ Al- le- lu- ja, ⟨al- le- lu- ja,⟩ al- le- lu- ja, ⟨al- le-
A
Trb. 1
al- le- lu- ja! ⟨Al- le- lu- ja, al- le- lu- ja, al- le- lu- ja, al- le-
T
Trb. 2
al- le- lu- ja! ⟨Al- le- lu- ja, al- le- lu- ja,⟩ al- le- lu- ja, ⟨al- le-
B
al- le- lu- ja! Al- le- lu- ja, al- le- lu- ja, al- le- lu- ja, al- le-
Vne.
B.c.

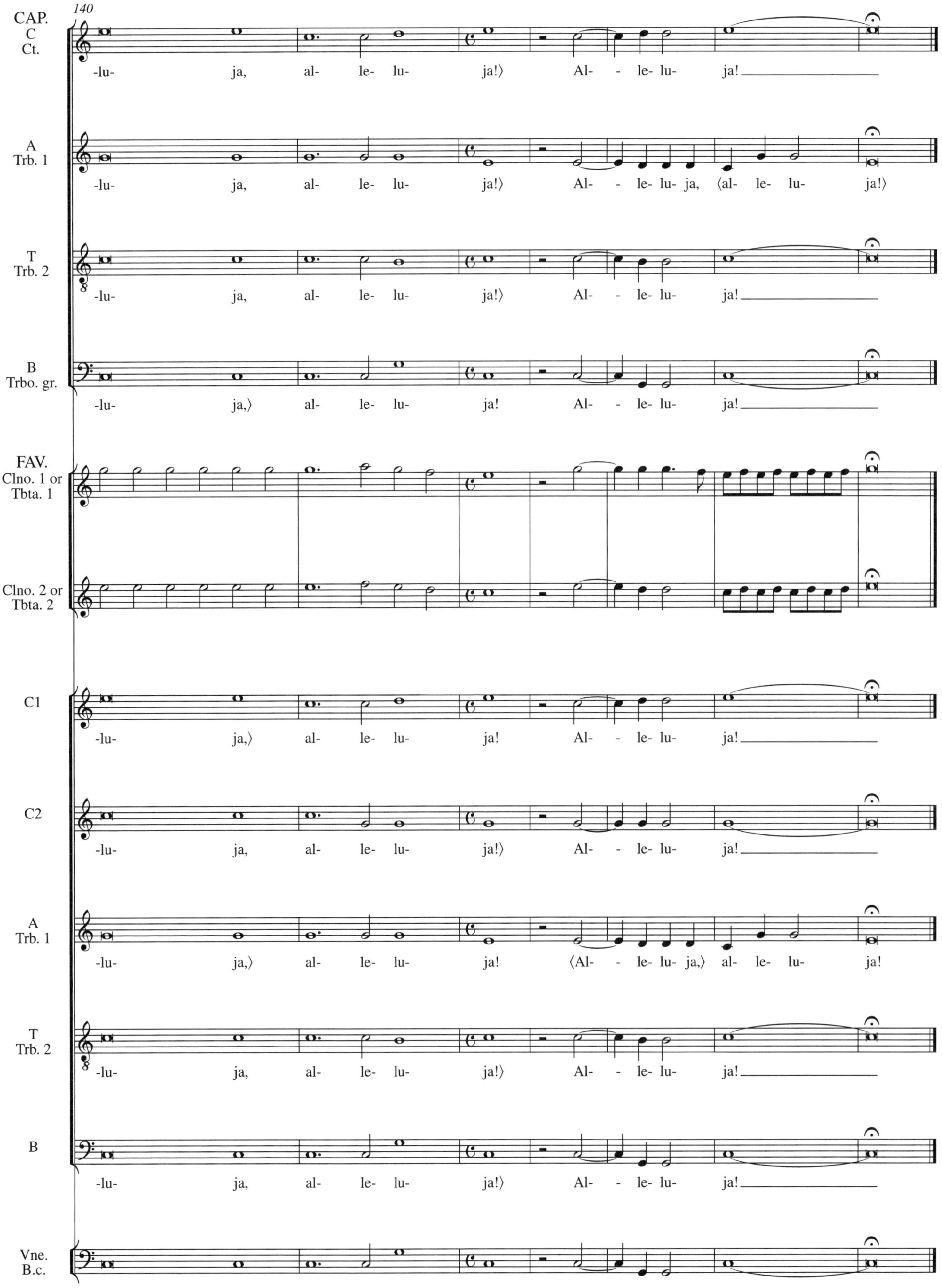

Vater Abraham

CAPELLEN
- Cantus 1 — Symphonia
- Cantus 2
- Altus
- Tenor Trombona — [Trombona]
- Bassus Bombardo

FAVORITEN
- Violino 1 — Symphonia
- Violino 2
- Violino 3
- Viola
- Violone 1
- Altus
- Bassus
- Violone 2 / Basso continuo

122

FAV.
A
-bar- me dich mein und sen- de La- za- rum, daß er das Eu- ser-ste sei- nes
Vne. 2
B.c.
FAV.
A
Fin-gers ins Was-ser tau- che und küh- le mei- ne Zun- ge; denn ich lei- de Pein, ⟨denn ich lei- de
Vne. 2
B.c.
FAV.
A
Pein, denn ich lei- de Pein⟩ in die- ser Flam- men.
B
Ge- den- cke, den- cke,
Vne. 2
B.c.
CAP.
Trb.
FAV.
Vn. 1
Vn. 2
Vn. 3
Va.
Vne. 1
A
B
Sohn, daß du dein Guts, dein Guts emp- fan- gen hast,
Vne. 2
B.c.

Er- bar- me dich, ⟨er- bar- me dich, er- bar- me dich,⟩ er- bar- me dich mein.

ge- den-cke, den-cke, Sohn,

daß du dein Guts, dein Guts emp-fan-gen hast in dei- nem Le- ben, und

Lazarus dagegen hat Böses, Böses empfangen;

nun aber wird er

ge- trö- stet, und du wirst ge- pei- ni- get. Va- ter A- bra- ham,

69
CAP.
Trb.
FAV.
Vn. 1
Vn. 2
Vn. 3
Va.
Vne. 1
A
⟨Va- ter A- bra- ham,⟩
Vne. 2
B.c.
75
CAP.
Trb.
FAV.
Vn. 1
Vn. 2
Vn. 3
Va.
Vne. 1
A
Va- ter A- bra-ham, er- bar- me dich
Vne. 2
B.c.
80
FAV.
A
mein, denn ich lei- de Pein, ⟨denn ich lei- de Pein, denn ich lei- de Pein⟩ in die- ser
Vne. 2
B.c.

Flam- men.

Und über das alles ist zwischen uns und euch eine

grosse Klufft befestiget,

92
CAP.
Trb.
FAV.
Vn. 1
Vn. 2
Vn. 3
Va.
Vne. 1
A
Er- bar- - me dich mein, er- bar- me dich
B
und ü- ber das al- les ist
Vne. 2
B.c.
96
FAV.
A
mein, ⟨er- bar-
B
zwi- schen uns und euch ei- ne gros- se Klufft be- fe- - sti- get,
Vne. 2
B.c.
99
FAV.
A
- me dich mein,
B
daß die da wol- ten von hin- nen hin- ab- fah- ren zu euch, kön- nen nicht, ⟨kön- nen nicht, kön- nen
Vne. 2
B.c.

FAV.
A
B
Vne. 2
B.c.
103
er- bar- - me dich mein.⟩
nicht,⟩ und auch nicht von dan- nen, ⟨und auch nicht von dan- nen⟩ zu uns her-
107
So bitt ich dich, Va- ter, ⟨so bitt ich dich, Va- ter,⟩
-ü- ber- fah- ren.
111
Va- ter, sen- de La- za- rum, ⟨sen- de La- za- rum⟩ in mei- nes Va- ters Hauß;
115
denn ich ha- be noch fünff Brü- der, noch fünff Brü- der, noch fünff Brü- der, noch fünff Brü- der,
118
daß er ih- nen be- zeu- ge, ⟨daß er ih- nen be- zeu- ge,⟩ auff daß sie nicht auch kom- men
122
an die- sen Orth der Qual, auff daß sie nicht auch kom- men an die- sen Orth der

131

130
CAP.
C1
-phe- ten, ⟨sie ha- ben Mo- sen und die Pro- phe- ten;⟩ laß sie die- sel- bi- gen hö-
C2
-phe- ten, sie ha- ben Mo- sen und die Pro- phe- ten; laß sie die- sel- bi- gen hö-
A
-phe- ten, ⟨sie ha- ben Mo- sen und die Pro- phe- ten;⟩ laß sie die- sel- bi- gen hö-
T
Trb.
-phe- ten, sie ha- ben Mo- sen und die Pro- phe- ten;⟩ laß sie die- sel- bi- gen hö-
B
Bom.
-phe- ten, ⟨sie ha- ben Mo- sen und die Pro- phe- ten;⟩ laß sie die- sel- bi- gen hö-
FAV.
Vn. 1
Vn. 2
Vn. 3
Va.
Vne. 1
A
B
sie ha- ben Mo- sen und die Pro- phe- ten; laß sie die- sel- - bi- gen hö-
Vne. 2
B.c.
6 4 ♯

134
CAP.
C1
-ren.
C2
-ren.
A
-ren.
T
Trb.
-ren.
B
Bom.
-ren.
FAV.
Vn. 1
Vn. 2
Vn. 3
Va.
Vne. 1
A
Nein, nein, Va- ter A- bra-ham! Son- dern wenn ei- ner von den To- den zu ih- nen
B
-ren. Sie ha- ben
Vne. 2
B.c.
138
FAV.
A
ging, son- dern wenn ei- ner von den To- den zu ih- nen ging, so wür- den sie Bus- se
B
Mo- sen, ⟨sie ha- ben Mo- sen, sie ha- ben
Vne. 2
B.c.

142
CAP.
C1
Sie ha- ben Mo- sen und die Pro- phe- ten, ⟨sie ha- ben
C2
Sie ha- ben Mo- sen und die Pro- phe- ten, sie ha- ben
A
Sie ha- ben Mo- sen und die Pro- phe- ten, ⟨sie ha- ben
T
Trb.
Sie ha- ben Mo- sen und die Pro- phe- ten, sie ha- ben
B
Bom.
Sie ha- ben Mo- sen und die Pro- phe- ten, ⟨sie ha- ben
FAV.
Vn. 1
Vn. 2
Vn. 3
Va.
Vne. 1
A
thun, so wür- den sie Bus- se thun.
B
Mo- sen,⟩ sie ha- ben Mo- sen und die Pro- phe- ten, sie ha- ben Mo- sen
Vne. 2
B.c.
♯
5

146
CAP.
C1
Mo- sen und die Pro- phe- ten,⟩ sie ha- ben Mo- sen und die Pro- phe- ten; laß sie die-
C2
Mo- sen und die Pro- phe- ten, ⟨sie ha- ben Mo- sen und die Pro- phe- ten;⟩ laß sie die-
A
Mo- sen und die Pro- phe- ten,⟩ sie ha- ben Mo- sen und die Pro- phe- ten; laß sie die-
T
Trb.
Mo- sen und die Pro- phe- ten, sie ha- ben Mo- sen und die Pro- phe- ten; laß sie die-
B
Bom.
Mo- sen und die Pro- phe- ten,⟩ sie ha- ben Mo- sen und die Pro- phe- ten; laß sie die-
FAV.
Vn. 1
Vn. 2
Vn. 3
Va.
Vne. 1
A
B
und die Pro- phe- ten, sie ha- ben Mo- sen und die Pro- phe- ten; laß sie die- sel-
Vne. 2
B.c.

150
CAP.
C1
-sel- bi- gen hö- ren. Hö- ren sie Mo- sen und die Pro- phe- ten
C2
-sel- bi- gen hö- ren. Hö- ren sie Mo- sen und die Pro- phe- ten
A
-sel- bi- gen hö- ren. Hö- ren sie Mo- sen und die Pro- phe- ten
T
Trb.
-sel- bi- gen hö- ren. Hö- ren sie Mo- sen und die Pro- phe- ten
B
Bom.
-sel- bi- gen hö- ren. Hö- ren sie Mo- sen und die Pro- phe- ten
FAV.
Vn. 1
Vn. 2
Vn. 3
Va.
Vne. 1
A
Er- bar- me dich, er- bar- me dich mein,
B
- bi- gen hö- ren. Hö- ren sie Mo- sen und die Pro- phe- ten
Vne. 2
B.c.
6 4 ♯ 6 ♯

137

158
CAP.
C1
so wer- den sie auch nicht glau- ben, so wer- den sie auch nicht
C2
so wer- den sie auch nicht glau- ben, ⟨so wer- den sie auch nicht
A
so wer- den sie auch nicht glau- ben, so wer- den sie auch nicht
T
Trb.
so wer- den sie auch nicht glau- ben, so wer- den sie auch nicht
B
Bom.
so wer- den sie auch nicht glau- ben, so wer- den sie auch nicht
FAV.
Vn. 1
Vn. 2
Vn. 3
Va.
Vne. 1
A
-bar- me dich mein, er- bar- me dich, er- bar- me dich mein,
B
so wer- den sie auch nicht glau- ben, ⟨so wer- den sie auch nicht
Vne. 2
B.c.

139

140

141

Sheet music, measure 170.

Text in vocal parts (CAP. C1, C2, A, T/Trb., B/Bom. and FAV. B):

- C1: auch nicht glau- ben, je- mand von den To- den auff- er- stün- de.
- C2: auch [nicht] glau- ben, je- mand von den To- den auff- er- stün- de.
- A: auch nicht glau- ben, je- mand von den To- den auff- er- stün- de.
- T (Trb.): auch nicht glau- ben, je- mand von den To- den auff- er- stün- de.
- B (Bom.): auch nicht glau- ben, je- mand von den To- den auff- er- stün- de.
- FAV. B: auch nicht glau- ben, ob je- mand von den To- den auff- er- stün- de.

Figured bass (Vne. 2 / B.c.): [7] 6 [4] [4 3]

Es wird eine grosse Trübsal seyn

143

13
CAP.
Trbo. gr.
FAV.
Fl. 1
Fl. 2
Trb. 1
Trb. 2
B
ei- ne gros- se Trüb- sal seyn, ⟨es wird ei- ne gros- se Trüb- sal seyn,⟩ als
Vne. B.c.
17
CAP.
Trbo. gr.
FAV.
Fl. 1
Fl. 2
Trb. 1
Trb. 2
C1
O Je- su
C2
O Je- su
B
nicht ge- we- sen ist, als nicht ge- we- sen ist.
Vne. B.c.

FAV.
C1
Christ, du machst es lang, du machst es lang mit dei- nem Jüng- sten Ta- ge! Den Leu- ten
C2
Christ, du machst es lang, du machst es lang mit dei- nem Jüng- sten Ta- ge! Den Leu- ten
Vne.
B.c.
wird auff Er- den bang, auff Er- den bang von we- gen vie- ler Pla- ge. Kom doch, kom
wird auff Er- den bang, auff Er- den bang von we- gen vie- ler Pla- ge. Kom
doch, kom doch, kom doch, du Rich- ter groß, und mach uns in der Gna- den
doch, kom doch, kom doch, du Rich- ter groß, und mach uns in der Gna- den
loß von al- lem Ü- bel! A- men. Kom doch, kom doch, ⟨kom doch, kom
loß von al- lem Ü- bel! A- men. Kom doch, kom doch, kom
doch,⟩ du Rich- ter groß, und mach uns in der Gna- den loß von
doch, du Rich- ter groß, und mach uns in der Gna- den loß von

146

49
CAP.
Trbo. gr.
FAV.
Fl. 1
Fl. 2
Trb. 1
Trb. 2
B
von An- fang der Welt, der Welt biß her, von An- fang der Welt, der Welt biß
Vne.
B.c.
53
CAP.
Trbo. gr.
FAV.
Fl. 1
Fl. 2
Trb. 1
Trb. 2
B
her, und als auch nicht wer- den wird. Es wird
Vne.
B.c.

148

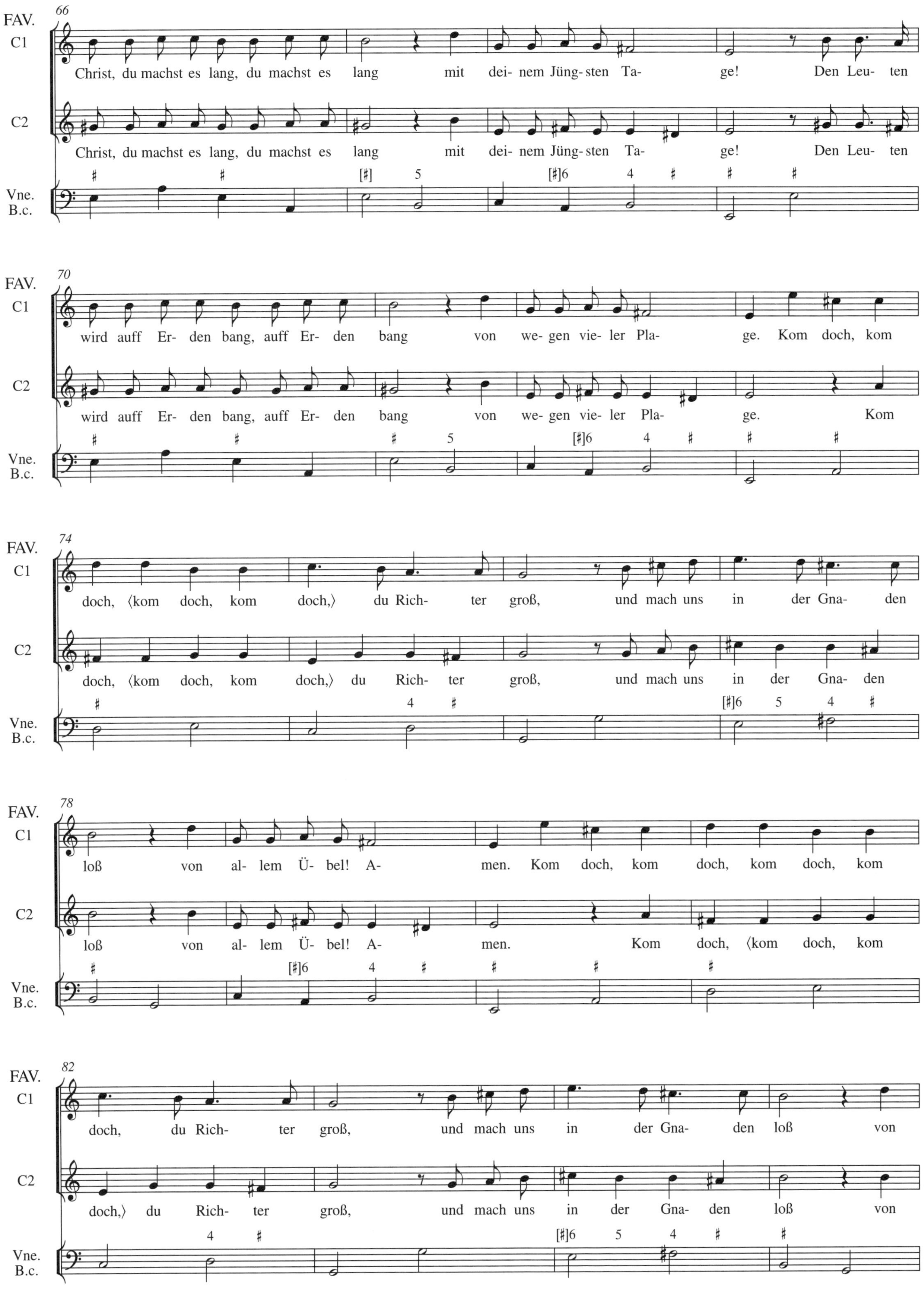

150

se- lig, und wo die Ta- ge nicht wür- den ver- kür- tzet, so wür- de kein Mensch

se- lig;

O Je- su Christ, du machst es lang mit dei- nem Jüng- sten Ta- ge! Kom doch, kom doch, du

O Je- su Christ, du machst es lang mit dei- nem Jüng- sten Ta- ge! Kom doch, ⟨kom doch,⟩ du

103
FAV.
C1
Rich- ter groß, kom doch, kom doch, du Rich- ter groß, kom doch, und mach uns in der Gna- den
C2
Rich- ter groß, kom doch, kom doch, du Rich- ter groß, kom doch, und mach uns in der Gna- den
Vne.
B.c.
106
CAP.
Trbo. gr.
FAV.
Fl. 1
Fl. 2
Trb. 1
Trb. 2
C1
loß, kom
C2
loß, kom
B
und wo die Ta- ge nicht wür- den ver- kür- tzet, so wür- de kein Mensch se- lig;
Vne.
B.c.
110
FAV.
C1
doch, kom doch, du Rich- ter groß, kom doch, und mach uns in der Gna- den loß.
C2
doch, kom doch, du Rich- ter groß, kom doch, und mach uns in der Gna- den loß.
B
umb der
Vne.
B.c.

Auß- er- wehl- ten wil- len wer- den die Ta- ge, die Ta- ge ver- kür- tzet, wer- den die Ta- ge, die Ta-ge ver-kür-tzet, umb der

Auß- er- wehl- ten wil- len wer- den die Ta- ge, die Ta- ge ver- kür- tzet.

CAP.
C
Ct.
120 Ripieno
O Je- su Christ, du machst es lang mit dei- nem Jüng- sten Ta- ge! Den
A
Trb. 1
O Je- su Christ, du machst es lang mit dei- nem Jüng- sten Ta- ge! Den
T
Trb. 2
O Je- su Christ, du machst es lang mit dei- nem Jüng- sten Ta- ge! Den
B
Trbo. gr.
O Je- su Christ, du machst es lang mit dei- nem Jüng- sten Ta- ge! Den
FAV.
Fl. 1
Ripieno
Fl. 2
Trb. 1
Trb. 2
C1
O Je- su Christ, du machst es lang mit dei- nem Jüng- sten Ta- ge! Den
C2
O Je- su Christ, du machst es lang mit dei- nem Jüng- sten Ta- ge! Den
C3
O Je- su Christ, du machst es lang mit dei- nem Jüng- sten Ta- ge! Den
C4
O Je- su Christ, du machst es lang mit dei- nem Jüng- sten Ta- ge! Den
A
O Je- su Christ, du machst es lang mit dei- nem Jüng- sten Ta- ge! Den
T
O Je- su Christ, du machst es lang mit dei- nem Jüng- sten Ta- ge! Den
B
O Je- su Christ, du machst es lang mit dei- nem Jüng- sten Ta- ge! Den
♭ ♯ ♯ ♯ 6 ♯ ♯
Vne.
B.c.

126
CAP.
C Ct.
Leu- ten wird auff Er- den bang von we- gen vie- ler Pla-
A Trb. 1
Leu- ten wird auff Er- den bang von we- gen vie- ler Pla-
T Trb. 2
Leu- ten wird auff Er- den bang von we- gen vie- ler Pla-
B Trbo. gr.
Leu- ten wird auff Er- den bang von we- gen vie- ler Pla-
FAV.
Fl. 1
Fl. 2
Trb. 1
Trb. 2
C1
Leu- ten wird auff Er- den bang von we- gen vie- - ler Pla-
C2
Leu- ten wird auff Er- den bang von we- gen vie- ler Pla-
C3
Leu- ten wird auff Er- den bang von we- gen vie- ler Pla-
C4
Leu- ten wird auff Er- den bang von we- gen vie- - ler Pla-
A
Leu- ten wird auff Er- den bang von we- gen vie- ler Pla-
T
Leu- ten wird auff Er- den bang von we- gen vie- - ler Pla-
B
Leu- ten wird auff Er- den bang von we- gen vie- ler Pla-
Vne. B.c.

131
CAP.
C Ct.
-ge. Kom doch, kom doch, du Rich- ter groß, kom doch, kom doch, du Rich- ter groß, kom doch, und
A Trb. 1
-ge. Kom doch, kom doch, du Rich- ter groß, kom doch, kom doch, du Rich- ter groß, kom doch, und
T Trb. 2
-ge. Kom doch, kom doch, du Rich- ter groß, kom doch, ⟨kom doch,⟩ du Rich- ter groß, kom doch, und
B Trbo. gr.
-ge. Kom doch, ⟨kom doch,⟩ du Rich- ter groß, kom doch, kom doch, du Rich- ter groß, kom doch, und
FAV.
Fl. 1
Fl. 2
Trb. 1
Trb. 2
C1
-ge. Kom doch, kom doch, du Rich- ter groß, kom doch, kom doch, du Rich- ter groß, kom doch, und
C2
-ge. Kom doch, kom doch, du Rich- ter groß, kom doch, kom doch, du Rich- ter groß, kom doch, und
C3
-ge. Kom doch, ⟨kom doch,⟩ du Rich- ter groß, kom doch, ⟨kom doch,⟩ du Rich- ter groß, kom doch, und
C4
-ge. Kom doch, kom doch, du Rich- ter groß, ⟨kom doch, kom doch, du Rich- ter groß,⟩ kom doch, und
A
-ge. Kom doch, kom doch, du Rich- ter groß, kom doch, kom doch, du Rich - ter groß, kom doch, und
T
-ge. Kom doch, kom doch, du Rich - ter groß, kom doch, kom doch, du Rich- ter groß, kom doch, und
B
-ge. Kom doch, kom doch, du Rich- ter groß, kom doch, kom doch, du Rich- ter groß, kom doch, und
Vne. B.c.

157

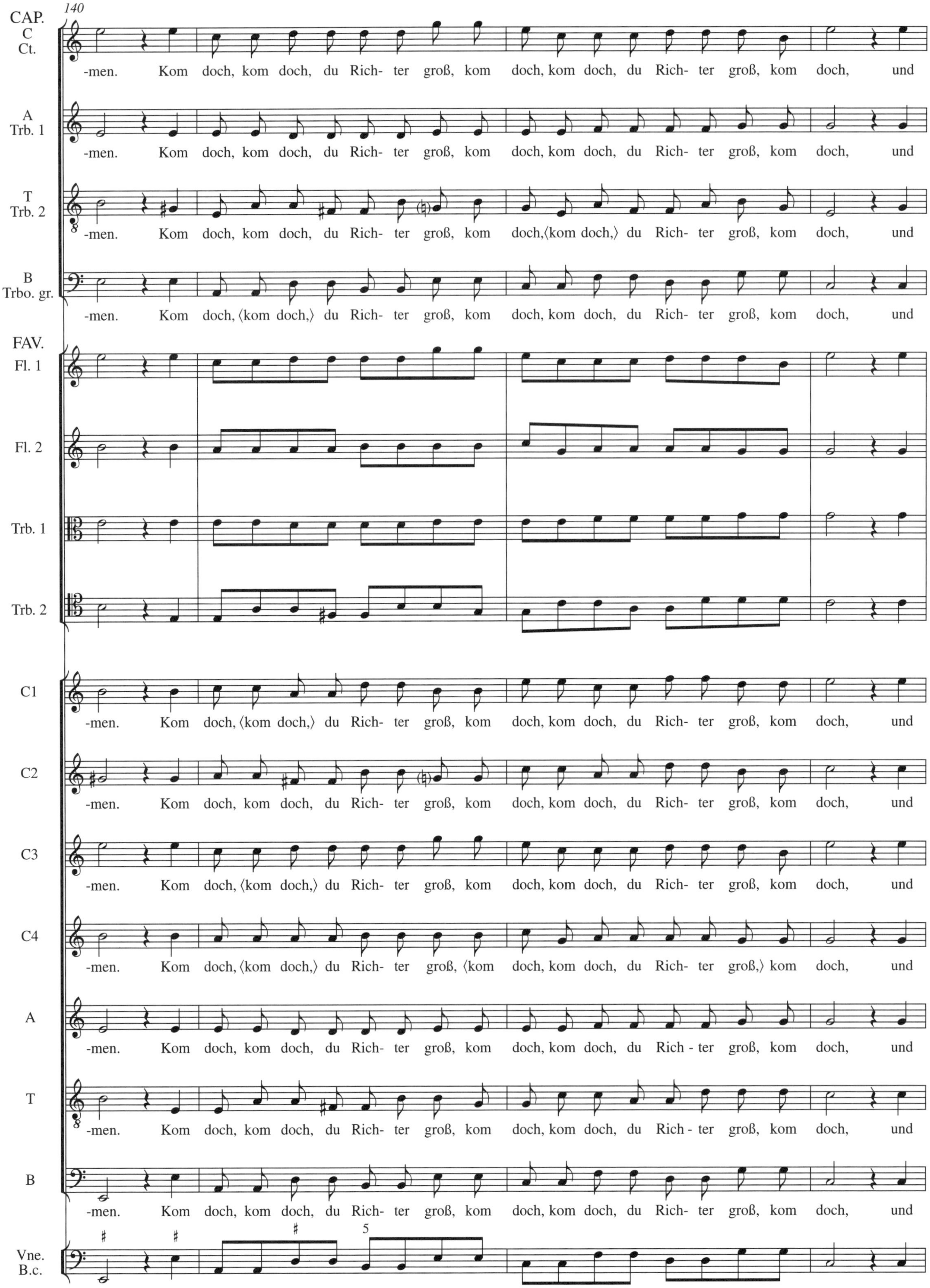

144
CAP.
C
Ct.
mach uns in der Gna- den loß von al- lem Ü- bel! A- men.
A
Trb. 1
mach uns in der Gna- den loß von al- lem Ü- bel! A- men.
T
Trb. 2
mach uns in der Gna- den loß von al- lem Ü- bel! A- men.
B
Trbo. gr.
mach uns in der Gna- den loß von al- lem Ü- bel! A- men.
FAV.
Fl. 1
Fl. 2
Trb. 1
Trb. 2
C1
mach uns in der Gna- den loß von al- lem Ü- bel! A- men.
C2
mach uns in der Gna- den loß von al- lem Ü- - bel! A- men.
C3
mach uns in der Gna- den loß von al- lem Ü- bel! A- men.
C4
mach uns in der Gna- den, Gna - den loß von al- lem Ü- bel! A- men.
A
mach uns in der Gna- den loß von al- lem Ü- bel! A- men, a - men.
T
mach uns in der Gna- den loß von al- lem Ü- bel! A- men.
B
mach uns in der Gna- den loß von al- lem Ü- bel! A- men.
Vne.
B.c.

Critical Report

Sources

Hammerschmidt's *Musicalische Gespräche über die Evangelia* was published as a set of nine partbooks in 1655 by the Dresden publisher Christian Bergen. Partbooks 1–6 were printed by Wolffgang Seyffert in Dresden; partbooks 7–9 by Georg Beuther in Freiberg. The partbooks are labeled as follows: Erste Stimme, Andere Stimme, Dritte Stimme, Vierdte Stimme, Fünffte Stimme, Sechste Stimme, Siebende Stimme, Achte Stimme, Neunte und letzte Stimme. Allowing for minor variations in punctuation, the title pages of the partbooks read as follows:

[Partbooks 1–5] Andreas Hammerschmidts | Musicalische Gespräche/ | über die | EUANGELIA, | Mit 4+ 5+ 6+ und 7+ Stimmen/ nebenst den | BASSO CONTINUO. | Erste [etc.] Stimme. | Mit Churfürstl. Durchl. zu Sachsen/ u. Freyheit | nicht nachzudrucken. | Dreßden/ Verlegts Christian Bergen/ und in | Wolffgang Seyfferts Druckerey gedruckt/ | Im Jahr 1655.

[Partbook 6] Andreas Hämerschmids [sic] | Musicalische Gespräche | über die | EVANGELIA | mit. 4. 5. 6. und. 7. Stimmen | nebenst dem | Baßocontinuo | Sechste Stimme | Mit Churf: Sachss: Freÿheit | Dreßden | Vorlegts Christian Bergen | Anno 1655.

[Partbooks 7–9] Andreas Hammerschmids | Musicalische Gespräche/ | über die | EVANGELIA, | Mit 4. 5. 6. und 7. Stimmen/ nebenst dem | BASSO CONTINUO. | Siebende [etc.] Stimme. | Mit Churfürstl. Durchl zu Sachsen / u. Freyheit | nicht nachzudrucken. | In Verlegung Christian Bergens Buchhändlers in Dreßden/ | Drucks Georg Beuther in Freybergk/ | Im Jahr 1655.

Partbook 6, the title page of which is shown as plate 1, includes the following additional text in the corners of the title page:

[Upper left corner] Ephes 5[:]19 | Redet unterein | ander von Psal, | men und Lobge- | sängen vnd Geist, | lichen Liedern

[Upper right corner] Eph: 5, 19. | Singet vnd | spielet den | HERREN | in ewrem | Hertzen

[Lower left corner] Cant. 11, 14. | Meine Freundin laß | mich hören deine Stim- | me denn deine Stimme | ist süße.

[Lower right corner] Cant. 11: 8: | Das ist die Stim, | -me, meines Freund

Partbook 6 also includes in an unlabeled corrigenda section just after the register:

Gönstiger Music-Freund/ Es sind dißmahl unter- | schiedene Fehler mit untergelauffen/ welche aber mit | grosser Mühe durch die Feder corrigiret worden; wird | sich ja noch was finden/ wollest du dienstlich gebethen | seyn/ selbige mit deiner bescheidenen Feder/ wie auch | im Texte vollends gut zumachen/ und sonderlich sol in | allen Stimmen vor dieses ₵ solches Signum C stehen. | ENDE.

Gracious Friend of Music: There are at this time various mistakes that have slipped in that have been corrected with the pen, however, with great trouble. If more are still to be found, you are officially directed to correct them completely yourself with your discreet pen, as also in the text. And especially, this sign C should stand in all parts instead of this sign ₵. End. (As translated in Harold Mueller, "The Musicalische Gespräche über die Evangelia of Andreas Hammerschmidt" [Ph.D. diss., University of Rochester, Eastman School of Music, 1956], 141.)

The principal source used for this edition is a complete set of nine partbooks located in Dresden, Sächsische Landesbibliothek – Staats- und Universitätsbibliothek, Musikabteilung, Mus Gri 39, 1 (RISM H 1948). Complete sets in Germany are also in Halle, Marktkirche Unser Lieben Frauen, Marienbibliothek; Wolfenbüttel, Herzog August Bibliothek, Handschriftensammlung; and Zittau, Christian-Weise-Bibliothek. Additional complete sets are in Brussels, Bibliothèque Royale Albert 1er/Koninklijke Bibliotheek Albert I, Section de la Musique; London, British Library; Rochester, N.Y., University of Rochester, Eastman School of Music, Sibley Music Library; Sibiu, Romania, Muzeul Naţional Bruckenthal, Biblioteca; Urbana, Ill., University of Illinois, Music Library; Växjö, Sweden, Landsbiblioteket; Vienna, Gesellschaft der Musikfreunde; Vienna, Österreichische Nationalbibliothek, Musiksammlung; and Zurich, Zentralbibliothek.

Incomplete sets and individual incomplete partbooks (shown by their number when provided by RISM, followed by the abbreviation "inc.") are available in Germany in Barth, Kirchenbibliothek (partbooks 2–5, 9); Berlin, Staatsbibliothek zu Berlin – Preußischer Kulturbesitz (1–5, 7–9); Brandenburg an der Havel, Domstift (1–8, 9 inc.); Detmold, Lippische Landesbibliothek (1 inc.); Dippoldiswalde, Evangelisch-Lutherisches

Pfarramt (1 inc.); Eisenach, Landeskirchenrat, Bibliothek (1, 2, and 5, each inc.); Glashütte, Evangelisch-Lutherisches Pfarramt, Pfarrarchiv (2–7, 9; partbook 3 lacks a title page and is completed by hand); Goslar, Marktkirchenbibliothek (1 inc., 6, 7 [2 copies], 8 [2 copies]); Herborn, Bibliothek des Theologischen Seminars (1–3, 5–6, 8–9); Leipzig, Musikbibliothek der Stadt (5); Luckau, Stadtkirche St. Nikolai, Kantoreiarchiv (1–8; 3 lacks a title page, 6 inc.); Lutherstadt Wittenberg, Stadtkirche, Pfarrarchiv (1–3, 6–8); Neustadt an der Orla, Evangelisch-Lutherische Kirchgemeinde, Pfarrarchiv (1–7, 9); Rudolstadt, Stadtbibliothek (5); Saalfeld, Thüringer Heimatmuseum, Bibliothek (1–9; 6 lacks a title page, 7 inc.); and Ulm, Stadtbibliothek (8). Additional incomplete sets are in Poland in Gdańsk, Biblioteka Gdańska Polskiej Akademii Nauk (1–2, 4–5, 7–9); Toruń, Uniwersytet Mikołaja Kopernika, Biblioteka Glowna, Oddział Zbiorów Muzycznych (1); and Wrocław, Biblioteka Uniwersytecka (1–5, 7–9; 4, 8 and 9 are inc.); in Sweden at Stockholm, Statens musikbibliotek (1–7; 1–6 are inc.) and Västerås, Stadsbibliotek (1–9; 2 inc.); and also at The Hague, Koninklijke Bibliotheek (2–9); Minneapolis, Minn., University of Minnesota Music Library (9 inc.); and Moscow, Rossiyskaya Gosudarstvennaya Biblioteka (inc.).

The *Ander Theil Geistlicher Gespräche über die Evangelia* was published as a set of nine partbooks by Dresden publisher Christian Bergen and printed by Wolffgang Seyffert (partbooks 1–6, 8, and 9) and Georg Beuther (partbook 7) in 1656. The partbooks are labeled as follows: Erste Stimme, Andre Stimme, Dritte Stimme, Vierdte Stimme, Fünffte Stimme, Sechste Stimme, Siebende Stimme, Achte Stimme, Neunte und letzte Stimme. The title pages read as follows:

[Partbooks 1–5, 8, and 9] Andreas Hammerschmidts | Ander Theil | Geistlicher Gespräche/ | über die | EUANGELIA, | Mit 5+ 6+ 7+ und 8+ Stimmen/ nebenst den | BASSO CONTINUO. | Erste [etc.] Stimme₊| Mit Churfürstl. Durchl. zu Sachsen/ u. Freyheit | nicht nachzudrucken₊ | Dreßden/ in Wolffg. Seyfferts Druckerey verfertigt/ und von | Christian Bergen verleget 1656.

[Partbook 6] Andreas Hammerschmidts | Ander Theil/ | Geistlicher Gespräche/ | über die | EUANGELIA, | Mit 5. 6. 7. und 8. Stimmen/ nebenst dem | BASSO CONTINUO. | Sechste Stimme. | Mit Churfürstl. Durchl. zu Sachsen/ u. Freyheit | nicht nachzudrucken./ | Dreßden/ in Verlegung Christian Bergens/ und in Wolffg. Seyfferts | Druckerey verfertigt/ 1656.

[Partbook 7] Andreas Hammerschmidts | Ander Theil | Geistlicher Gespräche/ | über die | EVANGELIA, | Mit 5. 6. 7. und 8. Stimmen/ nebenst dem | BASSO CONTINUO. | Siebende Stimme. | Mit Churfürstl. Durchl. zu Sachsen/ u. Freyheit | nicht nachzudrucken. | In Verlegung Christian Bergens Buchhändlers zu Dreßden/ | Druckts Georg Beuther in Freybergk. | Im Jahr 1656.

The principal source for the present edition is a complete set of nine partbooks located in Dresden, Sächsische Landesbibliothek – Staats- und Universitätsbibliothek, Musikabteilung, Mus Gri 39, 2 (RISM H 1949). Complete sets are also in Germany in Detmold, Lippische Landesbibliothek; Halle, Marktkirche Unser Lieben Frauen, Marienbibliothek; Wolfenbüttel, Herzog August Bibliothek, Handschriftensammlung; and Zittau, Christian-Weise-Bibliothek (first copy complete; second copy has only partbooks 1 and 9). Additional complete sets are in Brussels, Bibliothèque Royale Albert 1er/Koninklijke Bibliotheek Albert I, Section de la Musique; Rochester, N.Y., University of Rochester, Eastman School of Music, Sibley Music Library; Växjö, Sweden, Landsbiblioteket; Vienna, Gesellschaft der Musikfreunde; and Vienna, Österreichische Nationalbibliothek, Musiksammlung.

Incomplete sets in Germany are in Barth, Kirchenbibliothek (partbooks 2–5, 9); Berlin, Staatsbibliothek zu Berlin – Preußischer Kulturbesitz (1–6 and 9, of which 1, 2, 5, 6 are in second copy; also, the Staatsbibliothek [Mus. Ant. Pract. H 210ª] has 1–5, 7, 9); Brandenburg an der Havel, Domstift (1–6, 8–9); Eisenach, Landeskirchenrat, Bibliothek (1–4); Glashütte, Evangelisch-Lutherisches Pfarramt, Pfarrarchiv (2–7, 9); Goslar, Marktkirchenbibliothek (6–7, 9); Großmonra, Pfarrarchiv (9); Herborn, Bibliothek des Theologischen Seminars (1–3, 5–6, 8–9); Kassel, Gesamthochschul-Bibliothek, Landesbibliothek und Murhardsche Bibliothek, Musiksammlung (1–5, 7, 9); Luckau, Stadtkirche St. Nikolai, Kantoreiarchiv (1–8); Lutherstadt Wittenberg, Stadtkirche, Pfarrarchiv (1–3, 6–9); Rudolstadt, Stadtbibliothek (5); Saalfeld, Thüringer Heimatmuseum, Bibliothek (1–9; 7 inc.); and Schwerin, Landesbibliothek Mecklenburg-Vorpommern, Musikaliensammlung (7–9). Additional incomplete sets are in Poland in Gdańsk, Biblioteka Gdańska Polskiej Akademii Nauk (1–2, 4–5, 7–9); Toruń, Uniwersytet Mikołaja Kopernika, Biblioteka Glowna, Oddział Zbiorów Muzycznych (5); and Wrocław, Biblioteka Uniwersytecka (1–3, 5, 7, 9); in Sweden in Stockholm, Statens musikbibliotek (1–7; 1 and 5 are inc.); and Västerås, Stadsbibliotek (1–9; 8 inc.); and in London, British Library (1–8); Minneapolis, Minn., University of Minnesota Music Library (inc.); and Sibiu, Romania, Muzeul Naţional Bruckenthal, Biblioteca (4, 9).

The principal and unique source for the added capella parts is located in the Bohn Collection in Berlin, Staatsbibliothek zu Berlin – Preußischer Kulturbesitz, Ms. mus. 150, and consists of two sections. The first section, a package of loose manuscript pages wrapped in brown paper, contains performance parts measuring approximately 6½ × 8 inches. Each set of instrumental and vocal parts required by a work is gathered within a cover made from a sheet of 6½ × 16 inch paper that has been folded in half. Some covers contain two or three works. A title page for each piece or group of pieces within one cover states "CL" (the roman numeral of the manuscript collection, Mus. ms. 150) and the Bohn catalog number(s). Each page of every part is numbered on the recto.

The second section of Ms. mus. 150 is a bound book of organ tablatures in manuscript measuring 8 × 13½ inches. The title page for the organ tablatures states "Ms. mus CL. Partitur." The bound volume in which the organ tablatures are found is organized so that the tablature flows from the verso to the recto, with each new system indicated by a drawn horizontal line (see plates 5 and 6). This tablature is a score reduction of the original print and has not been used for this edition.

Editorial Methods

The eight works in this edition were selected to illustrate the different types of dialogues and instrumentations found in Hammerschmidt's *Gespräche,* as well as the various ways in which capellen were created to supplement and enlarge German Lutheran vocal works during the seventeenth century. Work titles have been taken from the registers of the 1655 and 1656 publications, with spelling and punctuation adjusted as necessary to conform to modern practices. Significant variants in titles are listed in the critical commentary. As instrumentation varies from work to work, the distribution of parts within the partbook sets is provided in the critical commentary. Though based on the sources, part names are editorial and appear without brackets; part names as they appear in the sources are reported in the critical commentary. Part names that appear as written directives in the source (such as those specifying a single instrument on a shared part) have been modernized without comment and added in brackets when missing from an individual part. Due to inconsistent labeling and text underlay in the capella parts, it is not always clear whether text underlay served as a cue to the instrumentalist or indicated that the part should be joined by a singer. In such cases, the label for the part name appears in brackets.

General written directives have been tacitly regularized, added when missing from an individual part, and placed above each group of staves (or above the staff when only applicable to a single part). Roman numerals have been changed to arabic, and abbreviations have been expanded without comment. Clefs have been modernized as needed, with the original clef provided as an incipit. Clefs also change as needed wherever an instrument and a voice share a part, using the modern vocal clef for passages with text underlay and the appropriate instrumental clef for untexted passages.

Many time signatures for triple meter have been modernized; original meter signs are noted in the critical commentary. The presentation of duple meter varies considerably both among the Hammerschmidt partbooks and between the Hammerschmidt prints and Bohn capella parts. While the majority of the Hammerschmidt partbooks notate duple meter in C, usually at least one partbook has ¢ instead. According to the corrigenda to the sixth partbook of the *Musicalische Gespräche* quoted above, Hammerschmidt intended for these passages to appear in C. The Bohn capella parts, by contrast, are always notated in ¢. For this edition, all passages in duple meter have been transcribed in C. The critical commentary reports all instances of ¢ in the Hammerschmidt partbooks, but not the Bohn capella parts.

The printed source has very few barlines except for an occasional single or thick barline at major structural divisions, and barlines in the Bohn parts are rare. When they appear in a majority of parts, single or single thick barlines have been tacitly converted to double barlines. Occasionally, a barline appears in only one or two parts (usually the basso continuo) to indicate the entry of a new vocal part; as these barlines function more as cues and often fall in the middle of a phrase, they have been omitted from the edition without comment. Other barlines in the sources are reported in the critical commentary; the term "stroke barline" refers to a very small handwritten barline as long as half the staff or less in Hammerschmidt's prints. Metric barlines have been tacitly added in the edition, as have final barlines at the end of each work.

Original note values have been retained, with two exceptions: all finals have been changed from a double longa to a breve with fermata, and notes that continue past a barline in the source have been divided into appropriate values and connected with a tie. Written directives for lengthy periods of rests, such as "94 Pausen," have been realized as rests without comment. The stem directions, beaming patterns, and rhythmic groupings of notes and rests in the source have been made to conform to modern conventions in the edition. Coloration is shown by open horizontal brackets. Slurs and braces that indicate melismas in vocal parts have been not been transcribed.

Accidentals made redundant by the use of modern barlines have been omitted without comment. Cautionary accidentals not provided by the source have been added in parentheses according to modern convention. Accidentals in the source that are rendered redundant due to the addition of an editorial accidental in the same measure have been removed and noted in the critical commentary. Although they appear unnecessary according to modern conventions, source cautionaries calling for a lowered third at the ends of phrases have been retained, as they would have been required by seventeenth-century performance practice. A ♭ or ♯ in the source that in modern notation is indicated by a ♮ has been altered without comment.

Continuo figures are original, even when ♯ or ♭ means ♮ in modern practice. Editorial figures appear in brackets. Repeated notes that have not been figured are assumed to have the same figure as the previous note in the same measure. Suspension cadences are assumed to be $\frac{5}{4}$–$\frac{5}{3}$; variants are clarified editorially. The note B in the bass is taken to imply a first inversion chord, whether or not the source consistently supplies the figure. However, whenever the figures ♯ or 5 appear above B, f♯ is assumed. Likewise, whenever 5 appears above an f♯, c♯ is assumed.

Archaic German spelling has been retained and made consistent within a work without comment. Spelling has not been made consistent between works. Modern spelling is selected only when the modern word appears significantly more times than the old or in at least once in two or more parts; the archaic German word is so outmoded as to render it unrecognizable; the source provides only a short form (for example, *dz* has been expanded to *daß*); the archaic spelling itself is inconsistent; and the modern syllables fit the underlay. Any other exceptions have been noted below. Capitalization, either necessary grammatically or unnecessary in text repetition, has been altered according to modern usage. Commas have been added between word or phrase repetition without comment. Repetitions of text shown in the original by an idem sign (*ij*) are enclosed in angle brackets in the edition. Editorial additions of text are enclosed in square brackets. Word divisions follow modern practices, except when archaic spellings with double consonants impede vocal diction.

Critical Commentary

The following critical commentary provides source information specific to each work and describes all textual and musical differences between the source and edition not otherwise covered above. The first two paragraphs in each "Sources" section below list the instrumentation of the nine Hammerschmidt partbooks, with partbook numbers appearing in parentheses, and describe general variations between source and edition. The next two paragraphs provide in folio order the contents of the capella parts (with part names used in the edition appearing in parentheses after part names found in the source), followed by information about the disposition of the capella parts within the Bohn collection and any general features of the source not reproduced in the edition.

Each "Notes" section describes specific differences between source and edition, with the abbreviations "Fav." and "Cap." used to clarify whether an instrument or voice belongs to the favoriten (Hammerschmidt partbooks) or capellen (Bohn capella parts). The following additional abbreviations are used in the paragraphs below: A = Altus; B = Bassus; B.c. = Basso continuo; Bom. = Bombardo; C = Cantus; Clno. = Clarino; Clav. = Clavicembalo; Ctin. = Cornetin; Ct. = Cornett; Fl. = Flauto; M(m). = measure(s); T = Tenor; Tbta. = Trombetta; Trb. = Trombona; Trbo. = Trombono; Trbo. gr. = Trombono grosso; Va. = Viola; Vn. = Violino; Vne. = Violone. A slash indicates alternative instrumentation, such as "Ctin. 1/Vn. 1." Shared parts are designated as "C & Ct." Notes are located in the score by measure number and part name. When specific notes and rests in a measure are cited, tied noteheads are numbered individually, and rests are counted separately from notes. Pitches are referred to using the system in which middle C = c'.

Freue dich, du Tochter Zion

SOURCES

Hammerschmidt partbooks. (1) Cornetin 1; (2) Cornetin 2; (3) Cantus 1; (4) Cantus 2; (5) Tenor; (6) Bassus; (7) No part; (8) Violon *Nach Beliebung* on title page; Continuus in part; (9) Continuus.

No. 1 in source. Register lists violins in place of the cornetins. Musical contents of the eighth and ninth partbooks are identical and are referred to together as B.c. in the notes. Most sections in triple meter notated ¢³₁; exceptions are reported below. Stroke barlines are in Cantus 1 (mm. 74–93) and Cantus 2 (mm. 74–92).

Bohn capella parts. Fol. 1r, 2 Cant: Voce è Cornett: (C & Ct.). Fol. 2r, Altús, Voce è Trombin: (A1 & Trb. 1). Fol. 3r, 2. Altús. Voce è Trombin: (A2 & Trb. 2). Fol. 4r, 2 Tenor, Voce è Trombon: (T & Trb. 3). Fol. 5r, 2 Bass: Voce è Trombono: (B & Trbo.). Fols. 1r–2r, organ tablature.

Catalogued as CL 1. Sections in triple meter notated ¢³₁.

NOTES

M. 1, B.c., meter is ¢³₁. M. 8, B.c., note 3, ¶ superimposed on figure 6. M. 16, Fav., C1, T, B.c., meter is ¢. M. 27, Fav., Ctin. 2/Vn. 2, rest is half rest. M. 27, Cap., A2 & Trb. 2, notes 1–6 are f'–f'–a'–a'–f'– f'. M. 28, Cap., A2 & Trb. 2, note 1 is f'. M. 34, Fav., T, notes 1–2, text is "einen." M. 40, Cap., A2 & Trb. 2, notes 1–6 are f'–f'–a'–a'–f'–f'. M. 41, Cap., A2 & Trb. 2, note 1 is f'. M. 46, Fav., C1, rip in page; note 4 flag and text missing. M. 51, Fav., C2, note 3, stem missing. M. 52, Fav., C1, rip in page; notes 1 and 2 and text missing. M. 56, B.c., meter is ¢³₁; "Freue dich." below staff. M. 69, Fav., Ctin. 1/Vn. 1, note 3 is e" with lines drawn to change it to f". M. 72, B.c., meter is ¢; "Sihe dein König." below staff. M. 72, Fav., ℀. M. 72, Cap., repeat sign faces both directions. M. 74, Fav., C1, rip in page; note 1 flag and text missing. M. 74, Cap., A1 & Trb. 1, note 1 is g♯'; note 6 is e' with lines drawn to change it to f♯'; A2 & Trb. 2, notes 2 and 4 are g♯'; note 5 is e♯'. M. 76, Cap., C & Ct., measure missing. M. 77, Fav., Ctin. 2/Vn. 2, note 3 is 16th note. M. 77, Cap., T & Trb. 3, note 6 is e. Mm. 80–100, Fav., C1 and C2, the heading of the second page of each cantus part indicates that these pages were printed in the opposite partbook. However, markings in each part indicate that the parts were performed as printed. Because this reversal of pages created two extra measures in C1 and two missing measures in C2, mm. 80–81 are crossed out by hand in the C1 part and written in the C2 part. This has been rectified in the edition by exchanging the second pages; page 2 of C1 (mm. 82–100) comes from book 4, while page 2 of C2 (mm. 80–100) comes from book 3; the two measures transferred from C1 to C2 in the source have been restored to C1. M. 82, Fav., T, notes 4–5, text is "einen." M. 93, B.c., B black whole note with lines drawn to change it to A whole note. M. 94, Cap., A2 & Trb. 2, note 4 is g' with lines drawn to change it to d'. M. 95, Fav., C2, note 4 is b'. M. 99, Fav., C2, note 4 is b'. M. 100, Fav. and Cap., no repeat sign.

Mein Sohn, warumb hast du uns das gethan?

SOURCES

Hammerschmidt partbooks. (1) Violino 1; (2) Violino 2; (3) Violino 3; (4) Cantus; (5) Altus; (6) Bassus; (7) Clavicimb. Violon.; (8) Violon *Nach Beliebung* on title page; Continuus in part; (9) Continuus.

No. 9 in source. Musical contents of the eighth and ninth partbooks are identical and are referred to together as B.c. in the notes.

Bohn capella parts. Fol. 21r, 2 Cantús. Voce è Cornett: (C2 & Ct. 2). Fol. 22v, 2 Altus. Voce è Trombin. (A & Trb. 1). Fol. 23v, 1 Cantús. Voce è Cornett: (C1 & Ct. 1). Fol. 25r, 1 Tenor. Voce è Trombon (T2 & Trb. 3). Fol. 26r, 2 Tenor. Voce è Trombon. (T3 & Trb. 4). Fol. 26v, Trombin. ([T1] & Trb. 2). Fol. 27r, 2 Bassús. Voce è Trombono. (B & Trbo.). Fols. 13v–15r, organ tablature.

Catalogued as CL 9 (title is *Mein Sohn, warúmb hastú unß daß gethan*) together with CL 6 (*Waß meinstu wil aúß*) and CL 10 (*Herr sie haben nicht Wein*). CL 6 and 9 parts share a single page (either recto or verso), with the former on the top half and the latter on the bottom. CL 10 parts are on the reverse sides of CL 6 and 9. The Trombin ([T1] & Trb. 2) part has a page to itself and names no voice, but it has text commencing m. 103.

NOTES

M. 1, Fav., Vn. 2, B.c., meter is ¢. M. 23, B.c., "Was ists:" below staff. M. 25, Fav., A, note 1, text is "hat." M. 26, Fav., A, note 2, text is "hat." M. 33, Fav., Vn. 3, two e" 8th notes between notes 3 and 4; crossed out by hand. M. 34, Fav., Vn. 2, rest is half rest. M. 48, Fav., Vne. 1 & Clav., note 1, figure 1 is ♭. M. 55, Cap., Trb. 2, notes 4, 5, and 6 are b with lines drawn to change pitch to a. M. 82, B.c., "Wisset ihr nicht" below staff. M. 84, Fav., Vne. 1 & Clav., figure is ♭. M. 93, Fav., Vn. 1, note 6 is a". M. 95, Fav., Vn. 1, meter is C^3_1; Vn. 2, A, B.c., meter is ϕ^3_1; B.c., "Alleluja." below staff. M. 103, Fav., A, note 5 is quarter note. M. 107, Fav., Vn. 2, note 3 is black whole note. M. 118, Cap., T2 & Trb. 3, notes 1 and 2 are tied (misplaced slur intended for notes 2 and 3). M. 119, Fav., Vn. 2, A, B.c., meter is ¢.

Herr, ich bin nicht werth

SOURCES

Hammerschmidt partbooks. (1) Trombona; (2) Tenor 1 â 6. Voc. Trombona; (3) Cantus 2; (4) Cantus 1; (5) Tenor 2; (6) Bassus; (7) No part; (8) Violon *Nach Beliebung* on title page; Continuus in part; (9) Continuus.

No. 11 in source. With the exception of some handwritten directives relating to vocal entries in the eighth partbook, the musical contents of the eighth and ninth partbooks are identical and are referred to together as B.c. in the notes. Partbook 2 lacks text; designation of Tenor 1 is a misprint. Partbooks 1, 2, and 5 have been transcribed as Trombona 1, Trombona 2, and Tenor in the edition. Trombona 1 and 2 have some handwritten or ruled barlines in the three sections that include rapid passages (mm. 1–8, 94–98, and 121–28). Text is "Tach" instead of "Dach" throughout.

Bohn capella parts. Fol. 37r, 1 Cantús. Voce è Cornett. (C1 & Ct. 1). Fol. 38r, 2 Cantús. Voce è Cornett: (C2 & Ct. 2). Fol. 39r, 2 Cantus. Cornett: (not transcribed). Fol. 40r, 1 Alt: Voce è Trombin: (A & Trb. 1). Fol. 41r, 1 Tenor. Voce è Trombon (T1 & Trb. 2). Fol. 42r, 2 Tenor: Voce è Trombon: (T2 & Trb. 3). Fols. 43r–v, 2 Bass: Voce è Bombardo. (B & Bom.). Fols. 16v–19r, organ tablature.

Catalogued as CL 11. The 2 Cantus. Cornett: part is identical to 2 Cantús. Voce è Cornett but lacks text. It has not been transcribed, as it is probably an extra performance copy for the cornettist.

NOTES

M. 1, Fav., Trb. 2, T, B.c., meter is ¢. M. 9, B.c., "HERR" below staff. Mm. 31–34, B.c., "HERR ich bin nicht werth." below staff. M. 84, Cap., B & Bom., "Tutti" below staff. M. 87, Cap., T1 & Trb. 2, half rest is missing. M. 88, Cap., T1 & Trb. 2, note 2 is c'. M. 118, B.c., figures are ♯-4-♯. M. 127, Fav., Trb. 1, barline between notes 6 and 7. M. 127, Cap., T2 & Trb. 3, notes 2 and 3 are quarter notes. M. 128, Cap., A & Trb. 1, notes 2–6 are e'–f♯'–g'–f♯'–e'.

O Herr hilf, wir verderben!

SOURCES

Hammerschmidt partbooks. (1) Altus; (2) Tenor; (3) Cantus 2; (4) Cantus 1; (5) Bassus 1; (6) Bassus 2; (7) No part; (8) Violon *Nach Beliebung* on title page; Continuus in part; (9) Continuus.

No. 12 in source. With the exception of some handwritten barlines in partbook 9, musical contents of the eighth and ninth partbooks are identical and are referred to together as B.c. in the notes. Handwritten, regular and/or stroke barlines appear inconsistently after mm. 8, 16, 17, 35, 51, 52, 70–76 and sporadically throughout mm. 90–104. It is not always clear whether some barlines are printed or handwritten (see the description of the corrigenda in partbook 6 under "Sources" at the beginning of the critical report). Text underlay of "O Herr" in a few instances has been altered editorially to "Herr hilf" for consistency.

Bohn capella parts. Fols. 44r–v, Tenor è Bass: (not transcribed). Fols. 45r–v, 1 Cantús. Cornett: (C1 & Ct. 1). Fols. 46r–v, 2 Cantus. Voce è Cornett: (C2 & Ct. 2). Fols. 47r–v, Altús. Voce è Trombin: (A & Trb. 1). Fols. 48r–v, 1 Tenor. Voce è Trombon: (T1 & Trb. 2). Fols. 49r–v, 2 Tenor. Voce è Trombon: (T2 & Trb. 3). Fols. 50r–v, 2 Bass: Voce è Bombardo: (B & Bom.). Fols. 51 r–v, 2 Cantús. Cornett: (not transcribed). Fols. 18v–21r, organ tablature.

Catalogued as CL 12. Text underlay of "O Herr" found in a few parts has been altered editorially to "Herr hilf" for consistency. C1 & Ct. 1 lacks text underlay from M. 59 to the end. There are two parts labeled "2 Cantus," which are identical except that 2 Cantus. Voce è Cornett: has text underlay and slurs, while 2 Cantús. Cornett has only a textual cue "Hallelúja:" below the staff at measure 97. Only the former has been transcribed. The Tenor è Bass part is a composite part consisting of the solo or most prominent sections of original print parts T1, B1 and B2. There are many tutti and solo directives above and below the staff in this part. It has not been transcribed, but it appears as plate 3 in this edition.

NOTES

M. 1, Fav., T, B.c., meter is ¢. M. 21, Fav., C1, note 1 is dotted quarter note. M. 22, Cap., T2 & Trb. 3, rest 2 is 8th rest. M. 24, Cap., B & Bom., rhythm is half rest, quarter rest, quarter note, 8th rest, 8th note. M. 41, Cap., T1 & Trb. 2, notes 1 and 2 are half notes. M. 52, Cap., B & Bom., rest missing. M. 64, Cap., T1 & Trb. 2, notes 2 and 3 are quarter notes. Mm. 77–91, text is "was ist das vor ein Mann, dem Wind und Meer gehorsam ist?" M. 89, Fav., C1, note 6 is a'; C2, four extra 8th notes g♯'–a'–b'–a' appear as notes 5–8 and are crossed out by hand; notes 2–4, text underlay is "dem Wind"; crossed out by hand; notes 3–4, handwritten text underlay is "ge-"; notes 5–8, text is "und Meer ge-." Mm. 89–90, Cap., C2 & Ct. 2, extra measures and some text underlay crossed out between these two measures; text underlay is "Das vor ein Mann." M. 92, Cap., T1 & Trb. 2, note is d'. M. 93, Cap., T2 & Trb. 3, text underlay is "Das ihm"; B & Bom., quarter rest missing. M. 97, Fav., C1, meter is $\frac{1}{2}$; B.c., meter is $\mathbb{C}^3_1$; C2, A, T, B1, B2, meter is $\frac{3}{1}$. M. 97, Cap., meter is $\frac{3}{1}$ in all parts. M. 104, Cap., A & Trb. 1, note 2 is quarter note. M. 105, Cap., A & Trb. 1, note 1 is f'. M. 106, Cap., C2 & Ct. 2, note 4 is c". M. 114, Fav., C1, A, T, B.c., meter is $\mathbb{C}$. M. 115, Fav., C2, note is b' with lines drawn to change it to a'; T, note 2, syllable is "-le-."

O Vater, aller Augen warten auff dich

Sources

Hammerschmidt partbooks. (1) Trombona; (2) Cantus 2; (3) No part; (4) Cantus 1; (5) Trombona; (6) Bassus; (7) No part; (8) Violon *Nach Beliebung* on title page; Continuus in part; (9) Continuus.

No. 20 in source. Musical contents of eighth and ninth partbooks are referred to together as B.c. in the notes. They are nearly identical, with the following exceptions in the ninth partbook: mm. 60 and 75, single thick barlines; mm. 61–83, handwritten or stroke barlines; mm. 55–56 and m. 71, measures crossed out; m. 72, rest 2 is handwritten quarter with two slashes below, each the length of a vertical space on the staff. Other regular or stroke barlines found frequently in Cantus 1 (mm. 17–75) and Cantus 2 (mm. 67–72). It is not always clear if regular barlines are printed or added by hand with a ruler. Continuo players may consider realizing more C-minor chords than the figures indicate.

Bohn capella parts. Fols. 196r–v, 2 Bassús, Trombono grosso. (B & Trbo. gr.) Fol. 197r, 1 Cantus. Voce è Cornett: (C1 & Ct. 1). Fol. 198r, 2 Cantus. Voce è Cornett: (C2 & Ct. 2). Fol. 199r, 1 Cantús. Cornett: (not transcribed). Fol. 200r, 2 Cantús. Cornett: (not transcribed). Fol. 201r, 1 Altús, Voce è Trombin: (A1 & Trb. 1). Fol. 202r, 2 Altús. Voce è Trombin: (A2 & Trb. 2). Fol. 203r, 2 Tenor. Voce è Trombon: (T & Trb. 3). Fols. 108v–110r, organ tablature.

Catalogued as CL 53 (title is *Aller Aúgen warten auff dich:*). 1 Cantus Cornett is identical to 1 Cantus. Voce è Cornett, and 2 Cantus Cornett is identical to 2 Cantus. Voce è Cornett, but each of the former parts lack text underlay and include only the single textual cue "Dancket dem:" below the staff in measure 102. Neither of these parts have been transcribed.

Notes

M. 1, B.c., meter is $\mathbb{C}$. Mm. 1–16, Fav., C1, C2, B, group rests crossed out by hand. M. 17, Cap., B & Trbo. gr., "Ô Vater aller Aúgen:" below staff. M. 44, Fav., B, note 1 is half note. Mm. 53–60, Fav., C1, C2, group rests crossed out by hand. M. 54, B.c., barline after note 1; note 2 crossed out. Mm. 55–59, B.c., lightly crossed out. M. 62, Fav., C2, notes 4 and 5 are tied (misplaced slur for notes 5 and 6). M. 63, Fav., C1, C2, whole note. M. 66, Fav., C1, C2, whole note. M. 70, Fav., C1, C2, whole note. M. 71, Fav., C2, rest missing; B.c., measure crossed out by hand. M. 75, B.c., handwritten fermata above and below thick barline. M. 83, B.c., note 2 is e♭. M. 83, Cap., B & Trbo. gr., note 2 is e♭. M. 90, Fav., C2, rest is half rest. M. 93, B.c., note 3, figure is 6. M. 102, Trb. 2, "Dancket dem." below staff; B.c., meter is $\mathbb{C}^3_1$. Mm. 102–4; Fav., Trb. 1, "Dancket dem HErren." below staff. M. 103, Cap., B & Trbo. gr., ends with barline with X above and N.B. below. Mm. 104–9, Cap., B & Trbo. gr., measures are below last staff of recto, framed by barlines, and marked with X above and N.B. below (see plate 4). M. 110, Cap., B & Trbo. gr., note crossed out before note 1. M. 111–12, Cap., C1 & Ct. 1, extra measures crossed out between these two measures. Mm. 113–17, Cap., B & Trbo. gr., "Denn er ist freundlich" crossed out below staff. M. 119, B.c., note 1, figure is ♭. M. 124, Fav., C1, whole note followed by 8th rest. M. 130, Cap., A2 & Trb. 2, notes 4–6 are f'–g'–f'. M. 132, Fav., C1, notes 2 and 3 are quarter notes with noteheads whited out. Mm. 132–33, Cap., A2 & Trb. 2, extra measures crossed out between these two measures. M. 137, Fav., C1, meter is $\mathbb{C}$. Mm. 140–41, Cap., B & Trbo. gr., extra measure crossed out between these two measures.

Gott fähret auff mit Jauchtzen!

Sources

Hammerschmidt partbooks. (1) Trombeta 1; (2) Trombona 2 on page 1 (misprint); Trombeta 2 on page 2; (3) Trombona & Voce; (4) Cantus 1; (5) Trombona & Voce; (6) Bassus; (7) Cantus 2; (8) Violon *Nach Beliebung* on title page; Continuus in part; (9) Continuus.

No. 28 in source; Trombona 1 & Voce misnumbered as no. 29. Register lists clarinos in place of the trombettas. Musical contents of eighth and ninth partbooks are identical and are referred to as B.c. in the notes. Partbooks 3 and 5 have been transcribed in the edition as Altus & Trombona 1 and Tenor & Trombona 2. While the part in the edition transcribed as Tenor & Trombona 2 includes designations for sections that require only the trombone, the Altus and Trombona 1 part lacks these directives; these designations appear in the edition with brackets. Some stroke barlines appear in the Clarino/Trombetta 1 (mm. 86–94; 101–3), Altus & Trombona 1 (mm. 24–28; 33; 46–53), sporadically throughout the B.c. (eighth partbook), as well as all through common time sections of C1.

Bohn capella parts. Fols. 73r–v, 1 Cantús. Voce è Cornett: (C & Ct.). Fols. 74r–v, 2 Altús. Voce è Trombin. (A & Trb. 1). Fols. 75r–v, Tenor. Voce è Trombon: (T & Trb. 2). Fols. 76r–v, Bassús. Voce è Trombono grosso. (B & Trbo. gr.). Fols. 36v–39r, organ tablature.

Catalogued as CL 21.

Notes

M. 1, Fav., Clno. 1/Tbta. 1, meter is $\mathbb{C}$. M. 1, Cap., A & Trb. 1, meter is $\mathbf{C}$. Mm. 7–14, Cap., Trb. 2, Trbo. gr., "Gott fähret auff:" below staff. M. 8, Cap., Trb. 2, fermata; Trbo. gr., fermata without dot. M. 12, B.c.,

"Frolocket." below staff. M. 44, B.c., "Er wird die Völcker." below staff. M. 53, Cap., C & Ct., rest missing. M. 54, Fav., T & Trb. 2, single thick barline between notes 2 and 3. M. 57, Fav., C1, note 3 is d″ with lines drawn to change it to e″. M. 58, Fav., C1, note 1 is e″ with lines drawn to change it to d″. M. 82, Cap., B & Trbo. gr., note 3 is half note. M. 95, Fav., C1, note 5 is dotted quarter note with notehead whited out. Mm. 95 (beat 3)–100 (beat 2), Cap., A & Trb. 1, measures missing. M. 100, Fav., C1, note 5 is dotted quarter note with notehead whited out. M. 105, B.c., "Alleluja." below staff. M. 116, Cap., T & Trb. 2, note 1 is d′. M. 118, Fav., C2, dotted whole note. M. 124, Fav., C2, note 1 is dotted whole note. M. 124, Fav., A & Trb. 1, rhythm is longa, half rest, whole rest. M. 130, Fav., C2, dotted whole note. M. 136, Fav., C2, dotted whole note. M. 140, Cap., A & Trb. 1, notes 1 and 2 are f′. M. 142, Fav., C1, B, meter is ¢. M. 143, Fav., B, note 1 is quarter note with notehead whited out. M. 144, Fav., C1, note 2 is c″ with lines drawn to change it to d″.

Vater Abraham

SOURCES

Hammerschmidt partbooks. (1) Cornetin 1 on page 1; Violino 1 on pages 2 and 3; Viol. in index; (2) Violino 2; (3) Violino 3; (4) Viola 4; (5) Altus; (6) Violon; (7) Bassus; (8) VIOLON *Nach Beliebung* on title page; Continuus in part; (9) Continuus.

No. 2 in source. Musical contents of eighth and ninth partbooks are identical and are referred to as B.c. in the notes. Partbook 6 is transcribed in the edition as Violone 1; partbook 8 as Violone 2 & Basso continuo.

Bohn capella parts. Fol. 80r, 2 Cantus. Voce. (C2). Fol. 81v, Altús. Voce. (A). Fol. 82v, 1 Cantus. Voce. (C1). Fol. 83v, 2 Bassús. . Voce è Bombardo: (B & Bom.). Fols. 84r–v, Tenor Voce è Trombon: (T & Trb.). Fols. 44v–47v, organ tablature.

Catalogued as CL 25 (title is *Vater Abraham*) together with CL 24 (*Heilig ist der Herr*). Pages are shared with CL 24 parts on the recto and CL 25 parts on the verso or vice versa.

NOTES

M. 3, Fav., Vn. 1, rhythm is half note, 8th rest, three 8th notes. M. 16, Cap., Trb., fermata. M. 70, Cap., Trb., notes are a with lines drawn to change them to g. M. 78, Fav., A, Vne. 1, meter is ¢. Mm. 118–20, Fav., A, text is "daß er ihnen bezeige." M. 131, Cap., A, notes 1 and 2 are e′ with lines drawn to change them to g′. Mm. 132–33, Cap., T & Trb., B & Bom., text is "dieselben," with two notes on final syllable. M. 133, Fav., Vn. 1, note 4, lowest staff line missing; note is a″, printed level to c‴. M. 146, Cap., T & Trb., note 5 is b with lines drawn to change it to a. M. 147, Cap., T & Trb., note 5 is c′ with lines drawn to change it to b. M. 148, Cap., T & Trb., notes 1 and 2 are c′ with lines drawn to change them to b. Mm. 149–50, Cap., T & Trb., B & Bom., text is "dieselben." M. 150, Fav., Vn. 1, note 3 is b″ but printed higher than neighboring c‴s, suggesting that d‴ was intended. M. 151, Fav., Vn. 1, note 1, lowest staff line missing; note is a″, printed level to c‴. M. 152, Cap., C1, rhythm is half rest, quarter rest, 8th note with tail erased to make it a quarter note, two 8th notes. M. 154, Fav., Vn. 1, note 1 is quarter note with notehead whited out. M. 155, Cap., C1, rhythm is half rest, quarter rest, quarter note, two 8th notes. M. 159, Cap., A, note 2 is a with lines drawn to change it to g. M. 167, Cap., B & Bom., measure crossed out, with X above and NB below; replacement measure appears after final measure of piece, again with X above and NB below. M. 169, Cap., B & Bom., rhythm is half rest, quarter rest, two quarter notes, two 8th notes. M. 170, Fav., A, fermata over group measures rest. M. 172, Fav., Va., note 5 is quarter note with notehead whited out.

Es wird eine grosse Trübsal seyn

SOURCES

Hammerschmidt partbooks. (1) Cantus 1; (2) Cantus 2; (3) Cantus 3. â 7. Voc. Flauto; (4) Cantus 6. [VI. *sic*] â 7. Voc. Flauto; (5) Trombona; (6) Trombona; (7) Bassus; (8) VIOLON *Nach Beliebung* on title page; Continuus in part; (9) Continuus.

No. 29 in source. Musical contents of Achte and Neundte Stimme are identical and are referred to as B.c. in the notes. Chorale text provided in flute and trombone parts commencing M. 120. Vocal and instrumental parts shared in partbooks 3, 4, 5, and 6 are given separate staves in the edition, with partbook 3 transcribed as both Cantus 3 and Flauto 1, partbook 4 as both Cantus 4 and Flauto 2, partbook 5 as both Altus and Trombona 1, and partbook 6 transcribed as both Tenor and Trombona 2.

Bohn capella parts. Fol. 84r, Ripieno: Cantús. Voce è Cornett. (C & Ct.). Fol. 85r, 2 Altus. Voce è Trombin. (A & Trb. 1). Fol. 86r, 2 Tenor. Voce è Tromb: (T & Trb. 2). Fols. 87r–v, Bassus. Voce e Trombonò grosso. (B & Trbo. gr.). Fols. 96v–99r, organ tablature.

Catalogued as CL 50.

NOTES

M. 1, Fav., C1, C2, C3, C4, Fl. 1, Fl. 2, meter is ¢. M. 7–8, Fav., Trb. 2, group measure rest is for 2½ measures. M. 20, Fav., Fl. 1, rhythm is half note, half rest. Mm. 20–21, B.c., "O JEsu Christ." below staff. M. 26, B.c., note 2, figure is 6. M. 65, Fav., Fl. 2, rhythm is half note, half rest. Mm. 65–66, B.c., "O JEsu." below staff. M. 91, Fav., Trb. 2, note 2 is b. M. 97, Cap., Trbo. grm., note 1 is 8th with tail scratched out. M. 98, Fav., C1, "Ripieno." below staff. M. 103, B.c., note 1, figure is ♯. M. 107, Cap., Trbo. gr., rhythm is half rest, 8th rest, four 8th notes, two 16th notes, one 8th note, two 16th notes. Mm. 119–20, Fav., single thick barline or regular barline in all parts at end of m. 119 and beginning of m. 120; "Ripieno" appears in space between measures. M. 120, B.c., "O JEsu." below staff. M. 120, Cap., B & Trbo. gr., "Tutti" below staff. M. 123, Cap., T & Trb. 2, note 4 is a. M. 128, B.c., note 1 is quarter note with notehead whited out. M. 129, Cap., A & Trb. 1, note 2 is e′ with lines drawn to change it to c′. M. 130, Cap., T & Trb. 2, note is half note. M. 132, Cap., T & Trb. 2, note 6 is g. M. 135, Cap., T & Trb. 2, note 2 is g with lines drawn to change it to a. M. 136, B.c., note 1, figures are ♯–4–♯. M. 138, Cap., T & Trb. 2, note 3 is g♯. M. 141, Cap., T & Trb. 2, note 6 is g. M. 145, B.c., note 1, figures are ♯–4–♯. M. 147, Cap., T & Trb. 2, note 3 is g♯.

DOES NOT CIRCULATE